THE POEMS OF CATULLUS

THE POEMS OF
CATULLUS

A Bilingual Edition

TRANSLATED WITH AN
INTRODUCTION BY
PETER WHIGHAM

UNIVERSITY OF CALIFORNIA PRESS
Berkeley and Los Angeles 1969

University of California Press
Berkeley and Los Angeles, California

This translation and introduction first
published in Penguin Books 1966
Copyright © 1966 by Peter Whigham

Library of Congress Catalog Card Number: 69-19556
Manufactured in the United States of America

To the memory of William Carlos Williams

CONTENTS

ACKNOWLEDGEMENTS

SOME of the poems originally appeared in *Artisan, The National Review, Agenda* and *Arion,* to whose editors I am indebted for permission to reprint them. Some also appeared in *Clear Lake Comes from Enjoyment,* Neville Spearman, 1959. Poem 61 was first printed in *The Marriage Rite,* The Ditchling Press, 1960. Both these books were written in collaboration with Denis Goacher.

In the specialised field of Catullan studies my debts are too widespread and diverse to be easily enumerated here. I can only hope that the book itself may in some sort prove a recompense for what I have pillaged from those more learned than myself. Unfortunately, C. J. Fordyce's *Catullus* (1961) did not appear until my work was more than half completed, but I have made what use of it I could. Burton and Smithers' curious but stimulating volume has been with me from the time when I began to make my first versions. Munro's *Criticisms and Elucidations of Catullus* (1878) and Robinson Ellis's Oxford Text, together with his *Commentary on Catullus* (2nd edn., 1889), have been my principal guides textually and exegetically. I have also used the texts of S. G. Owen (1893), Arthur Palmer (1896) and J. P. Postgate (1889). Mueller's text (1885) is of course incorporated in the Burton and Smithers volume. Salvatore Quasimodo's selected translation and Carlo Saggio's complete one have been an invaluable stimulus. I have also been helped by Ferrero's two studies (both Turin, 1955) and, perhaps most of all, by Noel's two-volume work: *Catulle* (An. XI – 1803), a fund of Renaissance and post-Renaissance lore on the subject of Catullus. From Landor's work as a

ACKNOWLEDGEMENTS

whole, and the second volume of his *Longer Prose Works* (Crump, edn. 1893) in particular, I have derived valuable, if somewhat idiosyncratic, insights. Finally, there has been my old edition (1797) of Lemprière, and Carnevale's *Roma Nel IIIe Secolo* (1896).

A year or so before his death, William Carlos Williams had some of these poems read to him. He handed them around among his friends. Not only his example as a poet but this practical encouragement of his as a master was a great help to me at a time when the book might well have been left in an incomplete state: '*hoc tibi, quod potui, confectum carmine munus/ pro multis, Alli, redditur officiis. . .*'.

Wine stains the verse;
the curse of time obliterates the arrogant line.

Then, in Verona, Campesani knows
the 'Roman hand':
"One woman could command
this song."
                    He sang
and fourteen hundred years
later, it reappears –
                    in the barrel's bung
(the hand that Campesani knows)
codex from wine-bung springing,
as from the dung
                    – the rose.

INTRODUCTION

WE know very little about Catullus's life: even the dates of his birth and death are uncertain. The likeliest figures are: born 84, died 54 B.C. His full name was Gaius Valerius Catullus. His father was a citizen of Verona and apparently of sufficient eminence to entertain Julius Caesar in his house. Either Catullus, or his family, owned a villa on the Sirmio peninsula on Lake Garda, about thirty miles west of Verona. We do not know where Catullus had his schooling, nor anything about his family, except that he had a brother who died before him. In poem 68 he tells us that already, at the age of 15 or 16, he had had his first experiences of love and, by implication, of poetry. In the same poem he describes Rome as his home and says that his life is passed there. We do not know when he left Verona, nor when he arrived in Rome nor where he lived when he was there. He speaks of a villa near Tivoli, but he must have had a town house as well. He constantly complains of being short of money, although he never seems wholly serious about this. He writes as a friend of Cicero and of many of the most distinguished figures of his day. He displays an aversion – again, less than completely serious – for Caesar and various members of his faction. He appears as one of the lovers of the notorious Clodia Metelli, and a leading figure – perhaps *the* leading figure – in the new movement in poetry. Sometime before 57 or 56 B.C. his brother must have died and been buried in the Troad, for it was in 57 that he, and probably his friend Gaius Cinna, accompanied C. Memmius Gemellus to Bithynia as members of his suite, and, according to the evidence of poem 101, Catullus paid a visit to his brother's grave when he was out there. A governor's term of office normally lasted a year, which means that poem 46 can be placed in the following spring when, if poem 4 is to be taken literally, Catullus returned to Italy in his own yacht, one that he had either bought, or perhaps had made, for the occasion. He appears to have sailed up the Adriatic and thence up the Po and the Mincio, or the Adige, to within a short distance of Lake Garda. The yacht was probably hauled the last few miles overland. In the poem, it is described as 'dedicated to quiet age', as though it were drawn up out of the water under the terrace of Catullus's villa, a memento to his eastern travels. There is no harm, however, in supposing that he still used it for sailing on the lake and entertaining the friends who visited him from Verona, or perhaps from Rome. Since poem 11 appears to contain a reference to Caesar's expeditions to Britain, it has been placed as late as 55 or 54 B.C. This would mean that he resumed his relationship with Lesbia after his return from Bithynia. The poem is often referred to as the last poem he addressed to her. But there is little direct evidence to support this. There is nothing to indicate that it comes after poems 107 or 109. Poem 10, one of his gayest and most light-hearted pieces of *boulevarderie*, also dates from this period. In short, the tradition that he died of what our grandmothers called 'a broken heart' finds no support in the poems. It is based solely on the assumption that his love for Clodia was of the conventional type of romantic – i.e. 'fatal' – passion. But I believe that many of the poems point to an altogether different and more complicated state of mind. All we can say for certain about his death is, that like his birth, it happened. He walks out of history, off the Roman scene, and in a very short while his book – or, more likely, his books – follow him, to be lost, to all effective purpose, for a thousand years. This, or something very like it, is the most we can say we know with reasonable certitude. The rest is conjecture, more or less plausible, and more or less harmful.

The conjecture starts, and, for the most part ends, with the dating of the poems from internal evidence. This provides a framework for an inferential web of motives and personal relations. Something like a biography in embryo begins to take shape. But poetry is not like history, and for a poet to say he has done this, or felt that, is about as unsure an indication as one would wish to have that he has in fact done the one or felt the other. Besides which, studies such as these are all too often used as a substitute for poetic understanding, rather than as an aid to it; and this is especially true of the Classics. Of course, any relic of a past civilisation has an extrinsic interest as part of a whole which it is the scholar's perfectly legitimate business to reassemble. From this point of view, no one can be anything but grateful for the labour that has gone into uncovering the minutiae of dates, deaths, offices and the cross-currents of relationships among Catullus's circle. However, in a volume devoted to the interpretation of his poetry, such findings should not be allowed to assume too great an importance: their true position is that of footnotes for the archaeologically curious. With this caveat in mind, it is with a certain amount of caution that I proceed to fill in as much of the historical background as seems to me more or less relevant, and that will allow me to move on to the dubious, and somewhat unfashionable, ground of biographical conjecture.

It is only reasonable to assume (the phrase is the King Charles's Head of Catullan biography) that the Lesbia of

[15]

Catullus's poems was Clodia Metelli. There is plenty of circumstantial evidence to support the identification, and nothing against it but the caution of scholars. She was the wife of Q. Metellus Celer, her cousin on her mother's side, and they lived in the Clivus Victoriae on the Palatine, the oldest and most exclusive residential area in the city. Celer was an old-fashioned if, apparently, able politician. He was a supporter of Cicero and the Senatorial party and was Roman praetor in the year of Cicero's consulship, which was also the year of the Catiline rebellion. After he had lost the consulship to Cicero, Catiline planned to have him assassinated; but the conspiracy failed and he fled to Etruria, where an army of malcontents left over from the Sullan proscription (freedmen, known from their liberator as *Cornelii*) was waiting for him. Gaius Antonius, Mark Antony's uncle, who had been elected to the consulship with Cicero, was sent to face the rebels from the south, while Metellus Celer, who on relinquishing his praetorship had been appointed Governor of Cisalpine Gaul, was despatched to Picenum, a district on the north-west coast of the Adriatic, where he was to raise troops, cross the Po and prevent the rebels retreating through the Alps. Antonius, who had originally supported the conspirators, declined at the last moment to lead his forces into battle, and it was actually his second-in-command, Marcus Petreius, who defeated and slew Catiline in the midwinter of that year (63–62), at Pistoria, the modern Pistoia, near Florence. Those of Catiline's followers who fled northwards across the Po and fell into Metellus Celer's hands were dealt with summarily as traitors. Celer remained in Cisalpine Gaul through the spring, summer and possibly autumn of 62. We do not know when he returned to

[16]

Rome, but it would certainly not have been before his
term of office was up. The province must, presumably,
have been in a state of some unrest, with dissident elements
using it as an escape route from the south. There is, of
course, no proof that he visited, or even knew, Catullus's
father; but the circle of influential or otherwise important
people in a provincial capital is necessarily small. He had
been of use to Caesar. (It is difficult to imagine Caesar using
his house unless he was.) And he could presumably be of
similar service to the new Provincial Governor, who would
certainly need help and advice from local dignitaries. If
Catullus had not yet left for Rome this could well have
been the source of his introduction to the circle of writers,
lawyers, politicians and well-bred opportunists who surrounded Metellus Celer's wife. It is almost certain★ that
Catullus's liaison with Clodia began before her husband's
death; and that was not far ahead. At whatever date the
Governor left the province, he must have been in Rome
well before his election as consul in 60 B.C. By the spring
of 59 he was dead.

The cause of his death is unknown; but it was common
talk that he had been poisoned by Clodia herself – as it was
that she had committed incest with her brother, Publius
Clodius, who had a house near hers on the Palatine. It
would appear that, during her husband's absence as Provincial Governor, Clodia's behaviour had become something more than a private scandal. Our source is Cicero's
Pro Caelio. It is the only full-length picture of her, apart
from what we are able to piece together from Catullus's
poems; and it is a vicious onslaught. Publius Clodius had

★ *Vide* poem 83 and, if the unnamed 'bright-shining goddess'
refers to Clodia, 68.

accused Marcus Caelius of being involved in the Catiline conspiracy and having seduced his sister. Cicero and Clodius were bitter enemies. The more violent of Caesar's faction felt that Cicero had betrayed them by going over to the Senatorial cause on his accession to the consulship. The charge was in fact true. But on top of this, Marcus Caelius was by way of being one of Cicero's more favoured pupils in the law courts. He had certainly been accepted – and later rejected – by Clodia as a lover; but to suggest that her honour had been impugned, and that restitution was therefore necessary, was ridiculous. Both the charge itself, and the ready defence by Cicero, were undoubtedly the result of the personal antagonism between the two men. The round went to Cicero. Marcus Caelius was acquitted, and the speech securing his acquittal was one of the most skilful and impassioned that Cicero ever made. Whether it gives a true, or even a just, picture of Clodia, is another matter. I do not believe that it does.

Cicero also lived in the Clivus Victoriae. The brilliant salons that one imagines Clodia to have held for the more attractive and interesting members of the popular party took place a few doors from his house. He did not have to rely on gossip to know the sort of power she was capable of wielding, or the influence she could exert. He knew, as a former colleague, the men who surrounded her. And the way he chose to destroy her was to make her appear ridiculous. This is something that Catullus, even in his fiercest moments, never does. Perhaps from Cicero's point of view she *was* ridiculous. He was certainly ill-equipped, temperamentally and as a man, to understand a woman of her sort. But more than this, she and her circle stood for a loosening of certain of the old values and, implicitly, a readjustment of woman's place in society. The ideal of the Greek *hetæra* was alien to Rome, and not one that Cicero could be expected to welcome. He had staked his career on the survival of the old ways and the predominance of the old aristocracy. To such a person, Clodia – or her example – might well have appeared less ridiculous than dangerous; and this would have been an added inducement to Cicero to take up the case. Whether or not he succeeded in destroying her, he certainly seems to have silenced her, for it is curious that after the trial she is to all intents and purposes never heard of again. She may have remarried and become a respectable Roman matron; she may have taken up permanent residence on a country estate. She may simply have died. Her exit is as enigmatic as Catullus's.

There is a theory that poem 49, in which Catullus thanks Cicero for some unspecified favour, refers to the *Pro Caelio* speech. It is possible, but, if true, was a short-sighted reaction on Catullus's part. Cicero's Clodia leaves us with little sympathy for anyone who should be so foolish – or tasteless – as to fall in love with her. The Clodia of the poems, taking the cycle as a whole, is worth the worst she can do to a man. Catullus may wish his experience at an end; he never regrets having had it. When Cicero speaks of Clodia he does so as a judge in the divorce courts faced with a particularly 'distasteful' case. There are few things men would sooner listen to than accounts of the scandalous behaviour of noble women, provided they themselves can remain at an unembarrassing distance and are thus free to express the moral judgements of their mood. It would be pleasant to think that our forefathers were more culpable in this respect than we are. At any rate, Cicero's words have proved as potent as Catullus's, and the disdain of his *Pro*

Caelio speech finds its echo in Noel's eighteenth-century French, but tinctured with the permissive smile of the voyeur.

' *Libre alors, elle donna, sans pudeur, carrière à tous ses goûts, et porta le mépris du blâme public, jusqu'à louer un jardin sur les rives du Tibre, pour choisir parmi les baigneurs ceux qui promettraient le plus à sa fougue érotique.*'

Whatever her real nature, this was the woman who had more effect on Catullus's life than perhaps anyone else. Nor is it necessary to admit to a conventionally 'romantic' relationship to recognise that he speaks to her in an altogether different and more disturbing tone from that in which he addresses the other women in his poems. When I come to discuss the *Attis* (poem 63), I shall try to show that it was precisely her forceful and sexually dominating character that attracted him. Which was exactly what repelled Cicero.

Finally, the question has to be faced whether she did in fact become a public prostitute. That Cicero should have said she behaved like one need mean little more than that, like the divorce court judge, he disapproved of her morals. Nor, except for two poems, would there be any need to take Catullus's own words very seriously. The forms which a man's feelings of self-disgust take when a woman's demands outstrip his abilities are familiar to most of us. But poems 37 and 58 do not readily lend themselves to such an interpretation. They are too specific.

The answer, I believe, lies in the peculiar and not uncommon vice of the well-born, the rich and the secure: the desire for low-life, poverty and insecurity. Poem 58 seems to me perfectly explicable on the assumption that

Clodia was the victim of *nostalgie de la boue*. She would not be the first well-brought-up young, or not so young, woman who has gone and stood on the street corners for kicks, not quite knowing herself how serious she was. But there is more to the poem than that. The 'cross-roads and back-alleys' of line 4 sound considerably less attractive than the elegance of Tiber-fringed gardens. The tradition being that she declined from the one to the other – a lesson to us all. But 'scions of Remus', which is the literal meaning of '*Remi nepotes*', is significant. It doesn't really read as though she took on all-comers. And '*glubit*' is odd, meaning to rub the husk off an ear of corn, and hence to masturbate. It does not imply full sexual relations, and it is not difficult to imagine the sort of squalid, and basically imitative, charade that she and some of her male friends may have indulged in. Perhaps the most striking thing in the whole poem is the violent juxtaposition of the words '*glubit*' and '*magnanimi*' in the last line. The effect is as though one should say in English that a man was 'pissed under the stars'. It is a fine rhetorical device, and one that I was not able fully to capture in my translation. Instead, I tried for an additional effect of my own, which was to broaden the implied irony by retaining the actual word 'magnanimous', though with its different meaning in English. The interesting point is that the depth of feeling in the poem comes in the first three lines, with their repetitions and shifting caesurae. Not at the end where one might expect it. The comparable lines in poem 11 (17–20) strike a much harsher and more despairing note. Beside them, '*glubit magnanimi Remi nepotes*' is like a rocket exploding.

There remains the evidence of poem 37. According to a

plain reading of the text, Clodia was to be found in a tavern
described as 'salacious' and frequented by the riff-raff of
the town, who went there to enjoy her favours. The
tavern in question is said to be 'nine pillars from the Temple
of the Dioscuri'. The word used for 'pillar' is '*pila*', which
refers specifically to a small pillar supporting a shop or
booth. *Columna* served for the grander, more ornamental
affair. Thus Catullus seems to have been indicating that one
should count the number of brothels, or low drinking-dens,
from the Temple of the Dioscuri. (This is a distinction that
I have not been able to make clear in my version.) When I
read the poem at first, I thought that this was all that I
needed to know, and that I understood Catullus's direc-
tions. For the rest, I was prepared to take the poem in the
same general sense as 58. But when I came to translate it I
realised that there was a puzzle in the expression, 'from the
Temple of the Dioscuri'. Why the Dioscuri? It told one
nothing, for there was no indication in which direction
one was to proceed. One could cross the Forum, in one
corner of which the Temple stood. Or go down the Via
Nova, beside it; or the Vicus Tuscus, behind it. It was not
until one day when I was hunting for odds and ends of
information about ancient Rome and turning the pages of
Carnevale's *Roma Nel IIIᵉ Secolo Dell'era Volgare* (1896), a
remarkably thorough survey of the Roman antiquities then
known, that I saw what I should have seen from the beginning, that the mention of the Temple of the Dioscuri
was a direct reference to Publius Clodius who, as is well
known, used it as a centre from which to deliver his
harangues and to create public disorders. The direction now
read, 'so many disreputable houses from the favourite'
stamping ground of Clodius and his henchmen, you will

find another disreputable house, where Clodia . . . etc.'.
Evidently, either Clodia's or Clodius's own house is intended. There is no means of knowing which. A reference
to a map of ancient Rome will show that the Clivus
Victoriae runs from the Via Nova up the Palatine, beginning almost opposite the Temple of the Dioscuri. We
are no longer required to believe that Clodia lived in a
brothel.

If I seem to have laboured this point it is because I believe
that the solution that I have offered is less inherently unlikely than that a woman of her background and, from
what we can understand of the poems, of her sexual tem-
perament, became in reality and earnest a prostitute. The
question will always remain open, and to an extent hinges
on what we understand by the word 'prostitute'. After all,
for Cicero a *hetæra* was a prostitute, and in his opinion
Clodia had stooped to become a form of *hetæra*, For
Catullus, if she slept with another man, she was a prostitute.
It may be asked, what chance did the woman have?

The date of Catullus's introduction into Roman society
is of interest in helping to assess how much of his younger,
formative life was spent in what he refers to as 'the province'. It is, unfortunately, likely to remain an unsolved
query. If Metellus Celer was responsible, Catullus would
not be likely to have left home before the spring of 62.
On the other hand, his father, who must have been a
wealthy man, was probably just as capable of arranging the
matter for himself. In which case, there is no knowing
when he left. There is a third alternative – of no help from
the point of view of dates, but worth considering for other
reasons. It is not impossible that he was provided with
introductions to Roman literary circles by Publius Valerius

Cato, the Veronese teacher, poet and critic, known not only to Catullus but to at least three other of the 'new poets', Ticidas, Gaius Cinna and Furius Bibaculus, all Cisalpines and all, at one time or another, pupils of his. It is likely, but unprovable, that Catullus was another. Cato was the author of a work on grammar, now lost, and probably of a poem called *Dirae*, which is still extant. A line of Cinna's refers to a poem called *Diana*, and a line of Ticidas', although not quite so certainly, to one called *Lydia*. Bibaculus speaks of him as though he were not only a master but an exemplar. He calls him 'the sole maker of poets', and laments the poverty of so discerning an individual. The warmth and personal element in Bibaculus's tributes, together with Catullus's poem (56), give us a hint of the mingled feelings of equality and respect which these men seem to have felt for him. If, as most scholars believe, Cato was the moving force behind the 'new poets', it would help to explain the number of Cisalpines among them. It would also explain, perhaps, something of the urgency and iconoclasm – although that word may be too strong – that they brought to their work. It would be misleading to suggest that, because they came from across the Po, an area which had not yet acquired full Roman status, they were what we should call 'provincials'. But there would be a freshness about them, and this – as in the case of Catullus – would give a bite to their Roman manners. Cato himself outlived all his pupils, dying as late as 25 B.C., only eight or nine years before Propertius, whose work, if he read it, he must certainly have approved of.

When we speak of the 'new poets' and the inspiration they derived from Cato, it should be remembered that we are in effect speaking of the work of Catullus and a tradition about Cato. The surviving fragments of the works of Calvus, Cinna, Cornificius, Bibaculus and Ticidas occupy barely three pages of print. Fortunately, in at least ten of his poems Catullus gives some very direct indications of what he and his friends felt about poetry, what their prejudices were and what they expected from it. Most of these poems are written to fellow poets and cast in the form of imaginary letters. (Catullus was fond of this convention: the opening lines of poem 13 follow the actual wording of a formal invitation to dinner.) Some of these 'letters' promise, or enclose, or make excuses for not enclosing translations of Greek models. Others are humorously abusive of poets of whom Catullus disapproves. Others are tributes to friends. We gather that the followers of the old-fashioned tradition of Roman epic were not popular with the 'new poets'; that long-windedness was to be avoided, and anything pompous, stilted or affected. We are told, or it is implied, that gaiety should be a concomitant of the arts, that the psychological and personal approach was to be preferred to the formal or public one, and that elegance (*venustas*), taste and learning (*doctrina*), were among a poet's most precious jewels. Perhaps the most illuminating poem of this genre is No. 50, where we see Calvus and Catullus, like any two poets who are also friends, playing at poetry together. We are aware that their poetry was a very close part of their lives. This was something new in Roman letters.

There is always the danger that the literary historian will invest the past with a more or less spurious unity. Life, we feel, is more haphazard than most biographers or historians would like it to appear. The documentary evidence for the idea that there was a new movement at all rests on three brief passages of Cicero, in one of which appears the term 'new poets' – and, as an ironic allusion to their literary ancestry, 'new poets' is written in Greek. To some people this has seemed insufficient proof of the existence of a literary movement, and they have consequently denied that the so-called 'new poets' worked together or formed a school. And yet one of the strongest impressions left from a reading of the dozen or so poems mentioned above is that Catullus, and the other writers with whom he mixed, felt themselves united, in an almost arrogant manner, *for* certain things in poetry, and *against* others, and this seems to me stronger evidence than Cicero's.

When Catullus started writing in 69 or 68 B.C. he had three traditions to draw on: Roman epic and tragedy; Roman comedy and satire; and the Roman love epigram, which was an importation from Alexandrian Greek. This third element was comparatively new, with a history of not more than fifty years. The examples we have are elegant but brittle; slight in accomplishment and small in quantity. The weightier traditions of tragedy and epic were not without Greek influence; but beside them the love epigram is like an exotic that had not taken root. By setting out these trends, in this way, I do not wish to imply that they were of equal importance, either in themselves or to Catullus. They were not. The exact nature of his debt to each is a matter of dispute. In general terms, however, it is safe to say that he drew his ability to convey grandeur (the Aegeus passage in poem 64) from the language of epic and tragedy; that he guessed at the uses to which colloquialism and realism might be put from the comico-satiric tradition; and that it was in the last, the somewhat precious form of the love epigram, that he saw the opportunity for original development. But a poet's greatness rests largely on the extent to which he is able to effect a synthesis of preceding traditions while producing something that has not been achieved before. This provides the fourth element: the constant and individual interplay between the three traditions. Fused in the *œuvre*, it is what gives Catullus's poetry its immediacy and, as far as Latin literature is concerned, its originality. Before Catullus, colloquialism had been confined to comedy; the elevated manner to epic or tragedy. In his poetry, for the first time, grandeur is heightened by un-expected realism. Colloquial diminutives express tender-ness, which rubs shoulders with an equally colloquial grossness. The subject matter of the Roman epigram is broadened and shifted to the entirely new field of the personal lyric with a wide variety of metres, many of which are used for the first time. As for his own epigrams, he confined these, for the most part, to elegiacs and, in so doing, made the brittleness of the epigrammatic technique, once a limitation of the poetic sensibility, an end in itself, so that his most vitriolic fantasies become disembodied and intellectualised: imagery and metaphor are discarded and a startling directness of language takes their place. But the most important thing Catullus does for the Alexandrian Greek epigram is to make it personal.

The Greek stimulus sought by the 'new poets' came mainly from Alexandria. The reason for this was natural enough. Ever since its foundation by Alexander in 332 B.C., and the subsequent building of the great library by Ptolemy I (323–283), it had been the principal centre of Greek cul-ture and learning. It represented what Greece meant to a con-temporary. It would be unrealistic to expect writers to have gone behind Alexandria to Greece itself. Her judgements

(in literary matters) were regarded as the judgements of
Greece, or the Greek cities. Added to this, Alexandria had,
in the second century B.C., come under Rome's sphere
of influence, and as recently as the year 80 had actually been
bequeathed to Rome by Ptolemy X in his will. The focal
point for the scholars and poets of Alexandria was, of
course, the magnificent library, the greatest in the world,
carefully nursed, for their own political ends, by the
Ptolemies. Callimachus himself, whom the 'new poets'
seem to have held in especial regard, worked and taught
there from c. 260 B.C. to his death in 250. Apollonius
Rhodius (c. 295–c. 230), whose *Argonautica*, so sympathetic
to modern tastes, was clearly known to Catullus, was a
pupil of his. This was where the 'new poets' derived their
ideal of the scholar-poet. It was here that they learnt to
attach as much importance to the complexity of a poet's
attitudes as to their consistency; it was here that they learnt
their love of allusion and the oblique manner, and to culti-
vate an almost eighteenth-century type of artistic sensibility. It was here they learnt their respect for craftsmanship
and their devotion to form and structure. But the 'new
poets' applied these Alexandrian principles and techniques
to a very un-Alexandrian situation. The Alexandrian
school had been engaged in resuscitating, and to some
degree had succeeded in embalming, an old tradition; the
'new poets' were endeavouring to found a new one.
When considering the Alexandrian school as a whole, it is
permissible to regret the lack of (apparent) spontaneity
which characterised the earlier age of the Greek lyric. But
spontaneity, or its appearance, is by no means the *sine qua
non* of a successful poem. We regret its absence only in
certain moods. To compare a poem of T. S. Eliot's to 'Go

Lovely Rose' and find Eliot wanting, is to indulge in an extra-literary judgement. Only a prejudice against Alexandrianism, as such, could lead us to deplore its deep and widespread influence over Catullus and his circle. They – or Catullus – had plenty of 'spontaneity', and if his more substantial works, such as poems 64 and 68, do at times read a little like *The Waste Land*, they seem none the worse for that.

The longer works (61–8) stand in the middle of the volume of his poems as it has come down to us, and deserve special mention. But first there is the volume itself, which is curiously arranged. It is in three parts: mixed lyrics, long poems and epigrams. The epigrams are nearly all quite short. Poem 76, the longest, runs to no more than twenty-six lines, and may more properly be called a love elegy. With 68, it represents the first example of its kind in Latin. This section is introduced, metrically, by the second half of the long poems, 65–8, which are all in elegiacs. The lyrics (1–60) are in various metres, sapphics, choliambics, iambic trimeters, and the metre which Catullus made peculiarly his own, the Phalaecian hendecasyllable, which appears to be calculatedly inserted between the others. Poem 34, the hymn to Diana, is the only one in this group to be written in glyconics, and, as with the elegiacs and poems 65–8, so here we find that the *first* of the long poems is also written in glyconics. It is clear that whoever arranged the poems did so on an almost exclusively metrical basis. This would suggest that the arrangement was at least post-Augustan. But the decisive factor is the length of the whole book – approximately 2,300 lines. This was enough to fill nearly three rolls; and the roll did not give place to our book form until the third or fourth century A.D. A likely theory is that poems 1–60 were originally a collection on their own, perhaps arranged by Catullus and preceded by the dedication to Cornelius Nepos. Various of the long poems, notably 64, would have been published as individual items, while the poems at the end may only have been passed round privately among intimates. There is no means of knowing whether they are complete, or whether they are a selection. While they contain some of Catullus's best and most characteristic work, they are of varying worth, and are certainly more scrappily arranged than the lyrics.

Turning to the long poems, we see that 61 is in the form of a personal epithalamium. Its recipient was Lucius Manlius Torquatus, a close friend of Catullus; about the wife we know nothing. Poem 62 is another epithalamium, but generalised. Taken with poem 34, it is one of the only two non-personal or public poems that he ever wrote. It is written in hexameters. Poem 63 is the celebrated *Attis*. The subject is again the relationship between male and female, but it is treated psychologically, in terms of Catullus's own experience, which he projects into the world of myth. It is written in the galliambic metre, so-called from the priests of Cybele, the *galli*, from whose ritual cries and dance movements it was said to be derived. It is the only poem to have survived in this metre either in Latin or Greek. Poem 64 blends each of the foregoing elements: it is mythological; love is a public, official affair (the marriage of Peleus and Thetis), and a private one (Ariadne's elopement, desertion and consolation). Like 62 it is in hexameters; they are the only two poems he wrote in this metre, and it will be seen that they neatly sandwich the unique galliambics. Poem 65 introduces three new subjects: poetry itself, friendship and the loss of his brother. It is a dedicatory epistle to 66 and is addressed to Q. Hortensius Hortalus. It

initiates the series written in elegiacs. Poem 66 itself is a
direct translation from a poem of Callimachus', an elegant
piece of court poetry verging on persiflage. Nothing – or
little – is accidental in Catullus, least of all the subject matter
of a translated poem. (Poem 51, his other direct translation,
is further proof of this.) In No. 66 he chose a poem in which
the protagonist – a woman's lock of hair – laments the fact
that it was severed from its mistress's head on her wedding
night, before she had had time to experience the pleasures
of married love. The lock recounts the occasion and its
circumstances, concluding with a request for votive offerings of the scents used by married women,* since it never
experienced these in life. If wives preface the 'chaste dalliance of the marriage bed' with libations such as these,
they will be blest with arts which will keep their husbands
faithful to them. I believe that Catullus has exaggerated the
element of persiflage that he found in the original and used
his subject matter as an opportunity to turn the poem he is
translating inside out and thus make a personal poem out
of a quasi official one. (Callimachus wrote the piece very
soon after the events which it describes.) Poem 67, set in
'the province', consists of a dialogue between Catullus and
the door of an unnamed woman. The Caecilius who is
spoken of as having right of access to the house may be the
fellow poet of No. 35, who had written a poem, presumably not unlike the *Peleus and Thetis*, on Cybele. Unfortunately, the local allusions are lost on us. We are
confronted with (at the least) incest and adultery, and an
attempt to swindle an inheritance out of someone under the
Lex Voconia, whereby a daughter was unable to inherit

* Married and unmarried women used different scents, just as they
wore their hair differently.

[31]

a substantial sum unless she produced a male child, in which case she could hold the money in trust. (The same reference is found in Poem 68.) The poem is amusing, coarse, realistic, and presents us with the obverse of 61 and 62. Poem 68 is addressed to Manlius Torquatus. I accept the theory that Manlius's wife, Aurunculeia, has died, and that the poem is principally one of consolation. But Manilus's love and loss is intricately interwoven with Catullus's own loss (of his brother) and love (of Lesbia). The themes of friendship and poetry make their reappearance. If 67 was local and realistic, 68 is local and romantic. Mythology is used again, but not now as a framework, as in 64. In 64 the mythological landscape was touched with realistic detail. Here, the world of reality is irradiated by myth. The poem has a trancelike quality.

Enough should have been said to show that this middle section contains poems that are essential to an understanding of Catullus, and that cannot be regarded separately from the rest of his work. If this seems a curious statement to the reader who has read my translations but is no Catullan scholar, then one of the purposes of my version will have been achieved. Not only do these poems form a unity in themselves but in their unreal and, in the *Attis*, violent and catastrophic, handling of the sexual relationship, they cast backwards to the extremes of tenderness, in the lyrics, and forwards to the obscenities of the Gellius sequence. (There are 'obscene' poems in section 1–60, and warm and tender poems in section 69–116; but as a generalization the distinction may be allowed to stand.) Catullus is, of course, a lyric poet. But, as far as the middle section is concerned 61 is nothing if not lyric; 65 and 68 both have very great lyrical beauty of a grave and meditative kind; while no man

should imagine he can fully apprehend the spirit which in-
forms the sparrow or the kissing poems, unless he has the
Attis in his other hand. The objection to the longer poems
would seem to resolve itself into an objection to 64. Since
64, together with 68, were doubtless the poems which he
himself regarded most highly, another look at both of
them would seem to be indicated.

Poem 64 is the centrepiece of the *Carmina*. It is a window
on the world of the gods. If to-day we look back over our
shoulders a thousand years or so we do not, even if we are
G. K. Chesterton Distributists, feel that we have missed-out
on Eden. But a similar idea does appear to have haunted
both Greeks and Romans round about the beginning of the
Christian era. It was no mere accident of literary fancy that
insisted that all genealogies, whether of city, state or hero,
should be traced back to the time when the gods still
walked the earth. This feeling was the inspiration of the
Evander passages in the *Aeneid*, of the whole of Ovid's
sprawling *Metamorphoses* and, of course, of the *Peleus and
Thetis*. Although the part played by Crete in the early
history of the Aegean basin was then unknown, it is plain
from both myth and legend that the Minoan age was in
some obscure way recognised as the time when this de-
sirable state obtained. In the *Peleus and Thetis* Catullus
employs all the resources of a highly eclectic and allusive
use of myth to depict its passing. In a sense, his method
allows him to have things both ways. He can pin-point
details which serve his purpose, but even while he is doing
this the body of the material he does *not* use still exerts its
influence over the reader's mind. Taking the Argonautic
expedition as a whole, the fact that Peleus leant over the
side of the ship and saw and fell in love with the sea-nymph

Thetis, is of such slight importance that it might well pass
unmentioned; while Ariadne, deserted on Naxos, and
Aegeus, committing suicide because of the wrong coloured
sail, are traditionally, and rightly, regarded as postscripts to
the Minotaur myth. Yet it is from the interlocking of
details such as these, taken from quite separate mythological
cycles, that Catullus conjures his orderly, consistent and
convincing narrative. His points of departure are pre-
Homeric Crete, the marriage of Peleus and Thetis, and
Troy. The connection between them is effected (backwards
to Crete) by the wedding quilt, and (forwards to Troy) by
the ill-omened epithalamium. We are shown how the fall
of Minoan Crete marked a process which, via the birth of
Achilles, found its conclusion in the fall of Troy. As though
this were not enough, Catullus also manages to tell us what
the golden age once meant in terms of human happiness
and what the future held in terms of human distress. He
describes how a goddess marries a man, and a woman
marries a god. A life of heroic action is rewarded in the
first instance, and love is eased of its passion in the second.
(Ariadne, as a victim of faithlessness and unrequited love, is
a mouthpiece for Catullus's own feelings.) He also shows
Nemesis overtaking evil (Aegeus's suicide), a foretaste of
the state into which the world is about to lapse. The way in
which the whole poem folds inwards on itself to the
seventy lines of Ariadne's lament, which represents the
'personal' centre of the poem, is perhaps best shown in
tabulated form.

ll. 1–49: The Argonautic expedition on which Peleus first
sees Thetis; the wedding day; the Palace; the coverlet on
the marriage bed.

ll. 50–264: Description of the scenes woven on the cover-let. This section is divisible as follows:

ll. 50–75: Ariadne on the beach at Naxos; the intrusion of evil in the shape of human faithlessness;

ll. 76–123: flashback of Theseus' expedition to Crete, the slaying of the Minotaur and Theseus' subsequent elopement with Ariadne;

ll. 124–31: return to Ariadne on Naxos;

ll. 132–201: Ariadne's lament and curse;

ll. 202–14: the Gods, as Theseus nears Greece, hear Ariadne's curse;

ll. 215–37: flashback of Aegeus's instructions to Theseus before he set sail for Crete, and Aegeus's feelings on that occasion;

ll. 238–48: return to the present; Theseus forgets his instructions; Aegeus commits suicide; Theseus' state of mind is compared to

ll. 249–50: that of Ariadne as she stands gazing out to sea after him;

ll. 251–64: the scene passes forward to the advent of Bacchus which ends the description of the coverlet.

ll. 265–77: Departure of the mortal guests.

ll. 278–304: Advent of the immortals – the Olympians, Jupiter and Juno, attended by the three demi-gods particularly associated with the bride and bridegroom. First: Chiron, the local deity of the chief mountain of Thessaly, Pelion, and the future tutor of Achilles; secondly, Peneus, spirit of the principal river and related to Thetis; and thirdly, Prometheus, who foreseeing the glory that will accrue from the marriage has persuaded Jupiter to sanction it. Apollo, who is to be the author of

[35]

Achilles' death, is mentioned as staying behind on Olympus.

ll. 305–22: Description of the Parcae.

ll. 323–81: Hymn of the Parcae, constituting the epithalamium; the scene moves forward as the Fates foretell the birth of Achilles and the subsequent fall of Troy.

ll. 382–408: Final peroration on the fallen state of man and the vanished golden age with which the poem has opened.

The total effect is cinematic. We have glimpses of paradisal landscapes emerging from the clear, primal world of sea and sky. But the clarity is deceptive and the landscapes and figures dissolve into one another and are never fully revealed. All is a little mysterious; which is as it should be; for without mystery there is no paradise.

The second of Catullus's Alexandrian pieces (68) is even more complex. Unfortunately, the text is very corrupt. We do not even know for certain whether it is one poem or two. (In the original codex, now lost, there was no indication where one poem ended and another began, and the copyist, after a break in his work, was quite capable of taking up his pen again at the wrong place.) It is unlikely that the string of queries which the poem prompts will ever be satisfactorily resolved. If it *is* one poem, is it addressed to 'Allius', or 'Mallius', and is this person identifiable with L. Manlius Torquatus of poem 61? Is the *domina* of the house which has been lent to Catullus for his meetings with Lesbia(?) its *châtelaine*, or Torquatus's mistress or both? And is his wife, Aurunculeia, dead? And is her death really the main subject of the poem or, more accurately, the core around which the poem is built? As elsewhere, I have taken different readings from different texts, and different suggestions from different scholars – usually I have found that it has been the more traditional interpretation that has attracted me – and having selected my material on the basis of what I found most stimulating poetically, I have then tried to rewrite the poem as I imagined Catullus might have written it had he been alive to-day and writing in English. As a poem is more than the sum of its constituent parts, a certain ruthlessness over details is often necessary. It is the whole poem which has to be captured and rewritten. One is, of course, grateful for whatever *donnés* fall into one's lap; *passim*. But the details of a poem are to be digested so that they become a part of the living grain of the new poem, not embalmed like flies in ointment. Since 68 is not a narrative poem, a table setting out the various strands of which it is composed will need to be a little more explanatory than was the case with 64.

ll. 1–40: Preface. Manlius has written to Catullus asking him for 'gifts of Love and the Muses' to console him in his sorrow. Catullus replies by saying that his own sorrows match Manlius's, and that he cannot comfort him as he would wish. Manlius's sorrow consists of the loss of his young wife, Aurunculeia; Catullus's of the loss of his brother.

ll. 41–73: Catullus nevertheless decides to record the debt that he owes to Manlius, who once provided him with a house in which he could meet Lesbia and in which they could make love. She comes to him as a 'bright-shining goddess'.

ll. 74–86: His own love for Lesbia, and the dead Aurunculeia's for Manlius are fused in the image of Laodamia, the symbol of wifely passion. (See Glossary.)

[37]

ll. 87–90: Troy, where Laodamia lost her husband, Protesilaus, is apostrophised in the first of two bridge passages as a source of widespread sorrow. (There may be a connection here with the 'historical' view of Troy expressed in 64, where its fall marks the end of the golden age.) Through Troy, Laodamia's loss is linked to Catullus's and so to Manlius's. In the intensity of her love she represents Aurunculeia, and of her grief, Manlius.

ll. 91–100: Catullus's brother was buried near Troy. The theme of his dead brother was broached in the first section of the poem; it is taken up again and expanded. Catullus repeats the original lines (20–4) nearly word for word.

ll. 101–4: The second of the bridge passages about the Trojan War. It is worth nòting that Helen is mentioned by name in the first, and Paris in the second. In themselves the two passages constitute a laconic reflection – from outside the body of the poem – on the inherently calamitous nature of mortal love.

ll. 105–30: Catullus passes from the cause of Laodamia's grief to an analysis of her love. He does this by means of three sustained similes, each to do with a different sort of bird: the Stymphalian birds of Hercules's Sixth Labour, the vulture, and mating doves. The poetic significance of the passage has puzzled commentators. Catullus's technique is similar to that of our seventeenth-century Metaphysicals. In lines 74–86, Laodamia's love is evoked in such a way that we are intended to participate in it; here the intention is that we should understand it. The passages complement each other.

To take the similes in order: I read the caverns under Mount Cyllene as a reference to the consummation of the marriage. Hercules can stand only for Manlius. We cannot know what his Sixth Labour suggested to a man of Catullus's day: but there can be no doubt that in the context of the poem the derivation of the word 'Stymphalus' (φαλλός and στύμα: the male and female members) is of peculiar significance. The reference to Hebe, goddess of eternal youth, whom Hercules marries on his apotheosis, indicates that Aurunculeia, still young, will be reunited with Manlius in the next world. In the second simile, the vulture symbolises death. The woman's gifts that the bride (Laodamia) brings will keep even death at bay. In the third simile, Isis's vulture gives place to Venus's doves which symbolise the enjoyment of sexual love. In brief, we have (*a*) ritualistic loss of virginity; (*b*) the expectations and the transforming power of love; (*c*) sexual pleasure.

ll. 131–48: Reintroduction of the theme of Catullus and Lesbia's love for each other. Their illicit relationship is compared with that of married love.

ll. 149–60: Epilogue. Catullus has, after all, written a poem to Manlius. Not a formal piece, such as he sent to Hortalus in 66, but an account of their relations with each other. The poem ends with a final evocation of Lesbia as 'she who endows Catullus with the quality of vision'.

I have often felt that the poem reads like an expansion of 65. Both poems consist of a similar, elaborate interweaving of the themes on which Catullus felt most deeply. Both have the same slow-trailing movement of successive clauses loosely drawn out. But what made the poem new in Latin, and remains its outstanding virtue, is the calculated and

[39]

delicate use of myth to delineate specific psychological states. It is a reminder of what we may well have lost in the works of Calvus, Cinna and the other 'new poets'.

There remains the *Attis*. Walter Savage Landor's comment with which he concludes his long survey of Doering's second edition of the *Carmina* (published nearly fifty years after his first, Leipzig, 1788) provides a fitting and amusing prelude to any discussion of the poem.

They who have listened, patiently and supinely, to the catarrhal songsters of goose-grazed commons, will be loth and ill-fitted to mount up with Catullus to the highest steeps in the forests of Ida, and will shudder at the music of the Corybantes in the temple of the Great Mother of the Gods.

The poem is a strange one, both violent and barbaric, full of odd coinings and archaisms, and written in the breakneck metre known as 'galliambic'. The youth Attis is described as crossing the sea to Asia Minor and there castrating himself in the frenzy of his devotion to the Mother Goddess. The act is accompanied in the original Latin by a change of gender. Attis calls to the other initiates of Cybele's cult to join him at her shrine on Mount Ida. There he falls into a coma. On waking, his immediate reaction is to regret what he has done. He returns to the beach and looks back over the sea. There follows a twenty-three-line lament for the civilised patrimony which he has abandoned. This patrimony is described in Greek terms, not Roman, a fact which has led some scholars to presume a Greek model, even a Greek original, and to read the whole as an expression of conflict between civilised and barbaric values. Even if such an interpretation is correct, it still leaves the core of the poem untouched. Following Attis's lament, Cybele unyokes one of her lions and instructs it to drive Attis back into the thickets on the slopes of Ida, where he is to remain for the rest of his life, a helpless devotee. In the last three lines, Catullus prays to Cybele to protect him from such desires; 'goad others to rabid madness; keep your fury from my house'. The lines are spoken as though he has woken from a nightmare (the preceding ninety lines) and recognised, with horror, himself in the figure of the unfortunate Attis. To emphasise this reading I have placed the last four lines of my version in direct quotes.

When considering the significance of this poem, I have always found it suggestive that the Temple of Cybele stood not far from Clodia's house, on the Palatine. The clashing cymbals, the drums and the peculiar ululating cries of the worshippers must on occasion have been audible to the members of Metellus Celer's household. Whether the initial stimulus that Catullus found in the myth lay simply in an accident of locality such as this, or whether it was the result of his trip to Asia Minor, it is impossible to say. The worship of Cybele had been introduced into Rome in the year 204 B.C., during the Second Punic War. A black stone representing the Goddess had been brought up the Tiber and placed, temporarily, in the Temple of Victoria, since the new temple which was designed to house it had not yet been completed. The cult was of Anatolian origin and was ecstatic like that of Dionysus, some of the terms being interchangeable. The general effect of both has been described as not unlike a latter-day Dervish dance. The worshippers inflicted wounds on themselves, were liable to despatch anyone who stumbled on their devotions, and, in the rites of the Mother Goddess, actually underwent voluntary castration. The fundamentally grave Romans viewed the cult with suspicion, and it was not allowed to spread.

On many occasions, in moments of intense emotion, Catullus expresses his feelings in the guise of a woman. The fact that homosexuality was not then considered either as a vice, an aberration or a disease, as it is now, is attendant but not cardinal to the point that I wish to make, which is that there was in Catullus a strain of femininity which went deeper than 'normal' adherence to the bisexual conventions of his class and time. His Iuventius poems strike exactly the same note as the heterosexual poems such as 32, that were not written to Clodia. The absence of 'guilt' is matched by a similar absence of 'spirituality' – of anything that is not a straightforward satisfaction of desire. With Clodia, lust is at a discount. It is she, to speak from the evidence of the poems, who displays the animality, not him. In No. 72 he even compares his feelings for her with those of a father for his daughter: an attitude unique in Roman poetry. Poem 51 is a translation from Sappho. It is the poem in which he gives Clodia the name of 'Lesbia'. In it, not only does he speak to her in the person of Sappho but the poem he has chosen to translate is one in which Sappho describes the physical sensations she experiences from the close presence of her beloved, in her case, if we accept the tradition, another woman. In the beautiful, tentacular 65, the startling, bright little vignette at the end (which is in itself a brilliant switch from the inclusive to the elliptical) represents an identification of himself with a young girl who is caught harbouring a guilty secret, the secret being her awareness of her own sexuality, symbolised by an apple. In poem 2, he wishes he were able to play with

[42]

Lesbia's sparrow, *as Lesbia does*, and imagines that if he were, he would feel like Atalanta, when she stooped to pick up the apple and so lost the foot-race and, with it, her virginity. In No. 66, we have observed how he assumes the *persona* of a woman's lock of hair; while in No. 68 we noted a similar switch of sexes in the passages where he describes Manlius's and his own grief in terms of Laodamia's. But there is an obverse to this side of Catullus's nature. It is to be found in his obsession with the more repulsive aspects of sexuality. (Poem 97 and the Gellius sequence.) His male drives found their outlet here, and the more disagreeable the news they could report, the more justification they provided for his invert fantasies. In poem 11 he refers to Lesbia as 'dragging the guts' out of him in the love act; and elsewhere there are references to the way in which a woman 'drains' a man of virility. It is as though Catullus felt that at the moment of orgasm a man became like Cybele's priests behind Metellus Celer's house. This I believe to have been the significance of the Attis myth for Catullus. Woman has, as it were, a lien on man's sex, an attitude expressed in the priests' castration and in the dramatic change of gender in the poem. It is the reason why Catullus was both repelled and attracted by the myth. The hate which Attis proclaims for Venus in line 17 is identical with that which Catullus in poem 85 expresses for Clodia. It has nothing to do with the antipathy of discordant elements, but arises from the repulsion from which attraction draws its strength, each succeeding the other in the love-hate see-saw. The experience is, of course, that of the manic depressive. And the *Attis*, as is now generally accepted, is a document of that state.

As a footnote to the poem, it is worth recalling the story

of how an ancestress of Clodia's vindicated her chastity by using her *zona* or girdle, to secure the image of the Holy Mother when the ship bringing it up the Tiber ran aground in shoal water. It is unclear exactly how she did this, but the garment in question was evidently used to bring the image (it was probably a meteorite) safely to dry land. Clodia must have known the tradition. And Catullus too. Did he perceive and, if so, relish, the irony it contained for him?

As I have intimated above, I have followed no one text in my translation. The original codex, which according to a venerable tradition was discovered wedging a wine barrel in Verona, at the end of the thirteenth century A. D., was in a poor state. There were frequent *lacunae* in the text, attributable (according to the same tradition) to the operation of the wine on the parchment. Worse than this, the codex itself disappeared again as mysteriously as it had appeared, although fortunately not before at least two copies had been taken. The efforts of scholars have since then been directed towards establishing the readings of this lost codex by collating the various copies – and copies of copies – which were taken from it. R. A. B. Mynors' recension is the most recent and among the most valuable contributions in this field. Unfortunately, as with C. J. Fordyce's volume, it appeared too late for me to make full use of it. Of the three almost certainly spurious poems, I have included No. 18, but followed Professor Mynors in omitting Nos. 19 and 20. Apart from this, I have taken 2b as part of 2 and have omitted 14b; I have taken 58b as part of 55; 78b as part of 78, and 95b as part of 95.

The hills around Lake Garda can have altered little since Catullus's day, and the waters of the lake not at all. Garda

is subject to very swift changes of weather. The wind off
the Dolomites blows down over Trento to Riva at the head
of the lake. The hills which stand close in to the northern
shore conduct the wind from one end of Garda to the other.
Suddenly the water will be curled into steep, crested waves,
so that the lake looks like the open sea. A very slight shift
of wind and the waters will be smooth again. The pleasure
boats which in the tourist season ply north and south between Riva, Malcesine and Desenzano wisely hug the
coast. The violent and abrupt changes of mood which
characterise the lake are also characteristic of Catullus's
poetry. They are each as unpredictable as the other. But the
lake could be called – is invariably and justly called –
'beautiful', and that is not the aptest word to apply to
Catullus's poetry. There is immediacy and vitality and
pathos and nobility. He riddles away with words, juggling
them about, a dozen times in half as many lines: eyes,
apples, stars, numbers and then more numbers. The primi-
tive is sometimes surprisingly near the surface. He has
made his own mirror, not of life but of himself, and in this
of course he is a Romantic. The tributes to him in English
poetry are innumerable. They start with Ben Jonson, and
go through Lovelace to Landor and Tennyson, Swin-
burne, Arthur Symons, Yeats and Ezra Pound. And when
I think how I shall conclude this tribute of mine, I turn
again to Walter Savage Landor whom I have just quoted
and whose paraphrases and adaptations stand second only
to those of Ben Jonson. The lines touch on the problem of
Catullus's 'obscenity'. Landor, whom no one could accuse
of laxity in this respect, saw that the question was of little or
no importance in itself, and existed only in an incidental
relationship to the whole work. The picture is a charming

one, and not without relevance in these days of hasty and intemperate opinions on the subject of what should and should not be printed.

> ' *Tell me not what too well I know*
> *About the bard of Sirmio –*
> *Yes, in Thalia's son*
> *Such stains there are – as when a Grace*
> *Sprinkles another's laughing face*
> *With nectar, and runs on.*'

St Briavels, Glos., 1944 –
Tirolo di Merano, 1965

As I have made clear on page 36 above, no one text served me through the writing of this book, or even through the rendering of any one poem. Robinson Ellis's text, however, was one of the first I began to use and was beside me throughout; it was, and still is, one of the more authoritative texts; and, looking back, it seems to me that I have probably consulted it more closely and more frequently than any other. Accordingly, it is the one that my publishers and I have decided, with the kind permission of the Oxford University Press, to use here.

Apart from the correction of a few missprints, the English text is the same as it is in the Penguin Classics series, where it first appeared.

THE POEMS OF CATULLUS

I

To whom should I present this
little book so carefully polished
but to you, Cornelius, who have always
been so tolerant of my verses,
                              you
who of us all has dared
to take the whole of human history
as his field
              – three doctoral and weighty volumes!
Accept my book, then, Cornelius
for what it's worth,
              and may the Muse herself
turn as tolerant an eye upon these songs
              in days to come.

[49]

2

Lesbia's sparrow!
                Lesbia's plaything!
in her lap or at her breast
when Catullus's desire
                gleams
and fancies playing at something,
                        perhaps precious,
a little solace for satiety
                when love has ebbed,
     you are invited to nip her finger
     you are coaxed into pecking sharply,
if I could play with you
                her sparrow
lifting like that my sorrow
                I should be eased
as the girl was of her virginity
when the miniature apple,
                gold/undid
her girl's girdle
          – too long tied.

3

Who loves beauty
                    veil her statues
veil Venus
            her attendant Cupids
Lesbia's plaything
                    Lesbia's sparrow
                                    is dead
dearer to her than her two eyes
sweeter than honey
                closer (even) than the young girl to her mother,
in her lap or at her breast
hopping from one shoulder to another
cheeping continually
                    to its mistress alone

. . . has now hopped solitarily
down that dark alleyway of no return
evil shadows of the underworld
                                Orcus
who swallows up all beautiful things
needless act! a small bird!
to close in on Lesbia's sparrow,

and swelling my girl's veiled eyes
                            which redden with tears.

4

My bean-pod boat you see here
     friends & guests
will tell you
     if you ask her
that she's been
     the fastest piece of timber
under oar or sail
     afloat.
Call as witness
     the rough Dalmatian coast
the little islands of the Cyclades
Colossan Rhodes
     the savage Bosphorus
the unpredictable surface of the Pontic Sea
where
     near Cytorus
before you were a yacht
you stood
     part of some wooded slope
where the leaves speak continuously in sibilants together.
Pontic Amastris
     Cytorus
– stifled with box-wood –
     these things
my boat affirms
     are common knowledge to you both.
More:
     you witnessed the beginning
     when she stood
straight on a hill-ridge behind the port,

in your waters
> you saw the new oar-blades first flash,
thence through the impetuous seas
carrying her owner
> the call
first to lee
> then to larboard
sometimes the wind-god falling full on the blown sheet.
Finally,
> no claim on the protection of any sea god
on the long voyage up to this clear lake.

These things have all gone by.
Drawn up here
> gathering quiet age
she dedicates herself gratefully to you
the heavenly twins
> Castor & Pollux
the Dioscuri.

5

Lesbia
live with me
& love me so
we'll laugh at all
the sour-faced strict-
ures of the wise.
This sun once set
will rise again,
when our sun sets
follows night &
an endless sleep.
Kiss me now a
thousand times &
now a hundred
more & then a
hundred & a
thousand more again
till with so many
hundred thousand
kisses you & I
shall both lose count
nor any can
from envy of
so much of kissing
put his finger
on the number
of sweet kisses
you of me &
I of you,
darling, have had.

6

Your most recent acquisition, Flavius,
must be as unattractive as
                              (doubtless) she is unacceptable
or you would surely have told us about her.
You are wrapped up with a whore to end all whores
and ashamed to confess it.
                              You do not spend bachelor nights.
Your divan, reeking of Syrian unguents,
draped with bouquets & blossoms etc.
                              proclaims it,
the pillows & bedclothes indented in several places,
a ceaseless jolting & straining of the framework
the shaky accompaniment to your sex parade.
Without more discretion your silence is pointless.
Attenuated thighs betray your preoccupation.
Whoever, whatever she is, good or bad,
                              tell us, my friend –
Catullus will lift the two of you & your love-acts into the
    heavens
in the happiest of his hendecasyllables.

7

Curious to learn
how many kiss-
es of your lips
might satisfy
my lust for you,
Lesbia, know
as many as
are grains of sand
between the oracle
of sweltering Jove
at Ammon &
the tomb of old
Battiades the First,
in Libya
where the silphium grows;
alternatively,
as many as
the sky has stars
at night shining
in quiet upon
the furtive loves
of mortal men,
as many kiss-
es of your lips
as these might slake
your own obsessed
Catullus, dear,
so many that
no prying eye
can keep the count

   nor spiteful tongue fix
   their total in
   a fatal formula.

8

Break off
        fallen Catullus
                time to cut losses,
bright days shone once,
        you followed a girl
                here & there
loved as no other
        perhaps
                shall be loved,
then was the time
        of love's *insouciance*,
                your lust as her will
matching.
        Bright days shone
                on both of you.
Now,
        a woman is unwilling.
                Follow suit
weak as you are
        no chasing of mirages
                no fallen love,
a clean break
        hard against the past.
                Not again, Lesbia.
No more.
        Catullus is clear.
                He won't miss you.
He won't crave it.
        It is cold.
                But you will whine.

You are ruined.
What will your life be?
Who will 'visit' your room?
Who uncover that beauty?
Whom will you love?
Whose girl will you be?
Whom kiss?
Whose lips bite?
Enough. Break.
Catullus.
Against the past.

9

Veraniolus,
first of friends,
have you returned
to your own roof
your close brothers
& your mother
still alive? In-
deed it's true you're
back again &
safe & sound
among us all.
So now I'll watch
& listen to your
anecdotes of
Spanish men &
Spanish places
told as only
you can tell them.
I shall embrace
your neck & kiss
you on the mouth
& on the eyes,
Veraniolus. . . .

Of all light-hearted
men & women
none is lighter-
hearted than Cat-
ullus is to-day.

10

Alfenus Varus
buttonholes me
in the Forum
where I'm lounging,
drags me off to
view a girl who
seems at first a
not unlady-
like young lady,
of obvious 'charms'.
The small talk turns
on how Bithynia
stands – my luck there.
I answer (which is
true) that neither
locals, praetors,
nor their aides
make money, that
palm-greasing's out,
that Memmius,
our praetor, greased
his aides elsewhere.
"But you," they said
"were not so poor
"you couldn't run
"to litter slaves –
"they come from there."
And I, because
of her, said lightly:
"Things were bad, but

"not as bad as
"that – I'd eight stout
"porters." (I, who've
no one, here or
there, even to
lift the foot of
my split pallet.)
And the girl, in
character, at
once cooed: "Lend me
"your porters for
"an hour or two
"this afternoon –
"I feel like doing
"what girls do,
"at Serap's shrine."
"My dear," I said,
"of course, but act-
"ually they're Gaius
"Cinna's – not my own
"– he lets me use
"them when I want.
"It's all the same. . . .
"You really mustn't
"take your friend's friends
"at their word,
                    young lady,
"it's common as
"well as comic."

II

Furius, Aurelius, friends of my youth,
whether I land up in the Far East,
where the long-drawn roll of the Indian Ocean
            thumps on the beach,
or whether I find myself surrounded by Hyrcanians,
the supple Arabs, Sacians, Parthian bowmen,
or in the land where the seven-tongued Nile
            colours the Middle Sea,
whether I scale the pinnacles of the Alps
viewing the monuments of Caesar triumphant,
the Rhine, the outlandish seas of
            the ultimate Britons,
whatever Fate has in store for me,
equally ready for anything,
I send Lesbia this valediction,
            succinctly discourteous:
live with your three hundred lovers,
open your legs to them all (simultaneously)
lovelessly dragging the guts out of each of them
            each time you do it,
blind to the love that I had for you
· once, and that you, tart, wantonly crushed
as the passing plough-blade slashes the flower
            at the field's edge.

12

While everyone else is laughing & drinking
you extend
        a surreptitious claw,
Asinius,
        towards the table napkins
of the negligent . . .
        an unattractive habit
you misguidedly think funny.
You demur?
        I assure you
it is at once squalid & unattractive.
Ask Pollionus, your brother
a boy crackling with wit
who would give a substantial sum
to disembarrass himself of your talents.
Expect, Asinius, a bombardo
of 300 hendecasyllables, or
return my napkin –
        of small value itself,
but a memory of friends,
        Veranius & Fabullus,
who sent this set of fine table linen
from Spain,
        a present cherished by Catullus
as his own Veraniolus –
as Fabullus mine – must always be.

13

I shall expect
you in to dine
a few days hence
Fabullus mine,
and we'll eat well
enough, my friend,
if you provide
the food & wine
& the girl, too,
pretty & willing.
I, Catullus,
promise you
wine & wit &
all the laughter
of the table
should you provide
whatever food
or wine you're able.
For, charmed Fabullus,
your old friend's purse
is empty now
of all but cobwebs!

In return, the
distillation
of Love's essence
take from me, or
whatever's more
attractive or
seductive than

[66]

Love's essence. For
Venus & her
Cupids gave my
girl an unguent,
this I'll give to
you, Fabullus, and
when you've smelt it
all you'll want the
gods to do is
make you one
gigantic nose
to smell it, always, with.

14

If, my irrepressible Calvus, I didn't
happen to love you more than my eyes
this hoax gift of yours would have made me
as cross as Vatinius. . . .
               What have I done to deserve
such (& so many) poets?
               I am utterly demoralised.
May the gods scowl on whoever
sent you this clutch of offenders
in the first place.
               – A grateful client?
I smell Sulla, the pedagogue.
A *recherché* & freshly culled volume,
such as this, could well come from his hands.
And that's as it should be – a meet &
acceptable sign that your efforts
(on his behalf) are not wasted.
But the collection itself is implacably bad.
And you, naturally, sent it along to Catullus
– your Saturnalian *bonne-bouche* –
so that Gaius, on this of all days,
might suffer the refinements of tedium.
No. Little Calvus. You won't run away
with this – for tomorrow, when the shops open,
I shall comb the bookstalls for Caesius, Aquinus,
Suffenus – all who excel in unpleasantness –
and compound your present with interest.
Until then, hence from my home, hence
by the ill-footed porter who brought you.
Parasites of our generation. Poets I blush for.

[68]

15

My love & I are yours to command
Aurelius –
        with the following 'modest' reservation:
if ever at any time you've held
a chaste good in your mind,
        unmarred by whatever desires,
modestly keep this boy of mine in like state.
I do not refer
        to the menace of common contacts,
to those set on their business
coming & going in the streets,
it is you
        & your punitive penis
I fear –
        a threat to all sorts & conditions of youth.
Wag this maleficent instrument
where, when & as much as you may
on whatever occasions occur
outside your domestic circle,
only withhold one item from its attentions. . . .
I present this modest request. But should
a congenital turpitude
        take you & prick you into
besetting Catullus's love with pitfalls of seduction
look for the luckless fate of the common adulterer:
he who
        with ankles clamped
and door open
        feels the horse-radish
(suitably cut for withdrawal)
        splitting him,
or the mullet's fins.

16

Pedicabo et irrumabo
Furius & Aurelius
      twin sodomites,
you have dared deduce *me* from my poems
which are lascivious
      which lack pudicity. . . .
The devoted poet remains in his own fashion chaste
his poems not necessarily so:
      they may well be
lascivious
      lacking in pudicity
stimulants (indeed) to prurience
      and not solely in boys
but those whose hirsute genitalia are not easily moved.

You read of those thousand kisses.
You deduced an effeminacy there.
You were wrong. Sodomites. Furius & Aurelius.
Pedicabo et irrumabo vos.

17

Cologna Veneta –
    where the good folk
dancing & holding their games
    at *festa* time
on the rickety bridge over the Gua
have fears of the crazy bridge-props
(cast-outs from the lumber yard)
slithering one day
    (plop) in the river-mud
– a bargain!
    A risible ruse on my behalf,
and a new little bridge
    your own *ponte di Catullo*
where even the cavorting priests of Mars
can play leap-frog in safety. . . .
    Pray, pitch
headlong from your precarious perch
where the marish mud waits deepest
    & blackest
& infinitely offensive
    a Veronese acquaintance of mine.
The man is a boor. His reflexes less
than those of a snoozing baby
rocked in the crook of its daddy's arms.
His bride's in her first flowering . . .
    a girl as capricious
as a pampered yearling,
    one to be watched
as closely as the tenderest grape-cluster . . .
while he,

for less than a fig,
yields her her maidenhead games
        wherever she wants them.
Nor has he 'risen to the occasion'.
        Hamstrung
like a Ligurian alder
        – the chopper's child –
in a ditch by the roadside,
        he responds precisely as though
no woman were anywhere near him.
The fool
    ·   hears nothing
sees nothing
        apparently knows nothing
(of himself included).
        Head over heels
from your little bridge
        despatch him
unawares –
        his dolt-like lethargy
traumatically stirred,
        who knows?
the husband may slough
        his horrid stupor
as the pack-mule casts
        its iron-soled slipper
in the obstinate mud.

18

I dedicate, I consecrate this grove to thee,
Priapus, whose home & woodlands are at Lampsacus;
there, among the coastal cities of the Hellespont,
they chiefly worship thee:
> their shores are rich in oysters!

21

Impresario of neediness
       to-day, to-morrow & of yesterday
Aurelius would openly stuff whom I love,
always with him
       laughing with him
'attached' to his flanks,
putting various tricks there to the test
– but in vain:
       schooled in your methods
I shall break you open (Aurelius) first. . . .
As a concomitance to good-living
       I acquiesce in your acts,
but when whom I love as honey,
       tastes your hunger
your thirst –
       preserve yourself. Desist.
You will attain your objective only
at the cost of being buggered by Catullus.

22

I must, Varus, tell you:
            Suffenus, known to us both as
a man of elegance, wit
            & sophistication
is also a poet
            who turns out verse by the yard.
No palimpsest copies
            but new books with new ivories
inscribed on Augustan Royal,
            the lines lead-ruled,
red tabs & red wrappers,
            the ends shaved with pumice.
But unwind the scroll
            & Suffenus
the well-known diner-out
            disappears.
A goatherd
            a country bumpkin
looks at us –
            strangely transmogrified.
What should one think?
            The envy of wits
becomes
            at the touch of the Muses
a bundle of gaucheries. . . .
            and he likes nothing better
fancies himself
            in the role of a poet. . . .
Yet who,
            in his own way,

is not a Suffenus?
> Each has his blind spot.
The moat & the beam.
> As Aesop says,
the pack on our own back
> that we don't see.

23

Friend Furius,
       'who has no slaves & no money' . . .
no bluebottle in the larder
       no spider
no bright hearth-fire,
       but a parent
& stepmother
       whose strong teeth
make short work
       of whatever you give them:
old boots & nails.
       Count yourself lucky –
your father, his lean spouse, yourself,
       in excellent health.
No indigestion.
       No fears of fire, flood & theft,
the usual bogies
       of prosperous householders.
(Who *could* want to poison you?)
       Your three bodies
like polished bone
       wonderfully dehydrated
by cold, heat & hunger,
       what more could you want?
Sweat, phlegm, saliva
       all nasal discharge
is foreign to you.
       You're as clean as whistles.
Even your arses, dry
       as fine, operative salt-cellars –

working
        maybe ten times a year,
the product
        like pebbles
or dry broad-beans
        easily friable
between the fingers
        & leaving no shit-smutch.
These blessings are not
        to be sneezed at.
You should count yourself lucky.
        You should also forgo
your importunate pleas
        for a 'small loan':
you've more than enough as it is
        – if you knew it.

24

Best sprig of the clan
  Iuventius
to-day, to-morrow, & of yesterday
rather you had bestowed the fortune
of Midas than your affections
on that man (Furius)
   'who has no slaves & no money'
"But he is *acceptable*, surely?" you query.
   – Indeed,
& this 'acceptable' man has no slaves, no money.
Dispute or disparage the point as you will . . .

  (the man still has no slaves,
  he still has no money).

25

From Thallus the pederast
        of flesh flabbier
than rabbit fur
        gooseskin
                earlap
or the cobwebby penis of an elderly gentleman,
from Thallus the pederast
        as rapacious as
a typhoon in winter –
        its crop of gaping sailors,
I demand
        my Spanish scarves
                my scrolls from Bithynia
which you have abstracted
        and of which you are making
ridiculous display
        as of family heirlooms.
Release my belongings from your glutinous clutches
or those fleshy thighs
        those slug fingers
may carry the acute inscriptions of the 'cat',
and you, afflicted by unwonted sensations,
find yourself tossed hideously about
        – a cockle shell on winter sea.

26

Your cottage, Furius, sheltered
from the dry Scirocco,
from Zephyrus,
            from Apeliota,
from the bitter North-East draughts
is exposed to an *over*draft of a different sort –
£1,250:
        ghastly . . . . ruinous.

27

Falernian,
　　　old Falernian!
cup-boy drown the cups
as custom of Postumia
tighter than the bursting grape
ordains
　　　but keep the water-jug
boon of the straight-faced
　　　　　　　　far hence
no friend to wine –
the Bacchus here is neat.

28

In Piso's suite
are empty pockets
empty trunks &
light equipage,
is that not so
Fabullus mine,
Veraniolus
best of friends?
Can you fill up
on his small beer?
can cash-books show
more gain than loss?
Or are you as
Catullus when,
a praetor's aide,
his cash-books showed
successive loss-
es, never gain?
Yes, Memmius, once
you filled me truly
slowly – daily –
with the length
of your great beam
and supine I
received it duly.
From what I see
your case is now
as mine was then:
you're stuffed with no
less large a crumb

of patronage. . . .
So, Veraniolus
& Fabullus
maledictions
on you both from
every Roman
god & goddess
for discredit
brought by you
upon the wolf-cubs
& their brood.

29

What man could stomach the sight
        that was not enthralled
by loot, lechery & the political game?
          Intolerable Mamurra
squanders
        what shaggy Gauls
what ultimate Britons
        once possessed.
Noblest Pederast!
        Your stomach remains unturned? . . .
You are enthralled by loot, lechery & the political game.
Overindulged & overweening
        the man stalks from bed to bed
like a white Venus-dove
        or a parody of Adonis.
Noblest Pederast!
        Does your stomach remain unturned? . . .
You are enthralled
        by loot, lechery & the political game.
Was this the reason for the British venture?
        That a debauched instrument
(yours & your son-in-law's)
        should gobble up all this money?
An unusual campaign . . .
        an unusual general!
Your celebrated munificence
        would appear to have been
'misplaced'. Has not enough coinage
        dribbled through this man's fist?
First his inheritance,

second the Pontic loot,
third, your own war in Spain,
      (the Tagus
where you washed for gold
      has a story of that),
& now Gaul,
      & now Britain,
shake in their shoes.
      Why keep him?
What is he good for –
      beyond treating the fattest endowment
as a comestible?
      Is this the reason
Rome's topmost tycoons,
      father-&-son-in-law,
have been playing billiards
      with our world?

30

Alfenus from Cremona
      forsakes the friendship of friends
friendless now
      quick to forget
            constant only in duplicity.
Gods of the Hill-Heavens do not smile on such acts,
a fact you ignore
      abandoning Catullus
fallen in sadness
      and ill.
            What can men do?
Where can a man hold fast?
      You commanded love
traduced my affections
      yielding no love-requital.
Now all is retracted,
      words, deeds,
dissolved under the clouds.
      You choose an eraser
but the gods will remember
      and Constancy also,
one day bringing the bitter herb to your mind.

31

Apple of islands, Sirmio, & bright peninsulas, set
in our soft-flowing lakes or in the folds of ocean,
with what delight delivered, safe & sound,

from Thynia
from Bithynia
you flash incredibly upon the darling eye.
What happier thought
than to dissolve
the mind of cares
the limbs from sojourning,
and to accept the down of one's own bed
under one's own roof
– held so long at heart . . .

and that one moment paying for all the rest.

So, Sirmio, with a woman's loveliness, gladly
echoing Garda's rippling lake-laughter,
and, laughing there, Catullus' house
catching the brilliant echoes!

32

Call me to you
at siesta
we'll make love
my gold & jewels
my treasure trove
my sweet Ipsíthilla,
when you invite
me lock no doors
nor change your mind
& step outside
but stay at home
& in your room
prepare yourself
to come nine times
straight off together,
in fact if you
should want it now
I'll come at once
for lolling on
the sofa here
with jutting cock
and stuffed with food
I'm ripe for stuffing
                              you,
my sweet Ipsíthilla.

33

Vibennius & son, renowned
among bath-hut pilferers
                    père
an adept at 'massage'
                    fils
of voracious if of hirsute buttocks
why not remove yourselves?
Those manual depredations
    are common knowledge,
the allurements of those bum-cheeks
    a drug on the market:
why not remove yourselves?

34

Moving in her radiant care
chaste men and girls moving
wholly in Diana's care
      hymn her in this.

Latona's daughter, greatest
of the Olympian race, dropped
at birth beneath the olive trees
      on Delian hills,

alive over mountain passes,
over green glades and
sequestered glens,
      – in the talkative burn,

Juno Lucina in the groans
of parturition, Hecat, fearful at crossed ways, the nymph
      of false moonlight.

You whose menstrual course
divides our year, stuff
the farmer's harvest barn
      with harvesting.

Sacred, by whatever name invoked
in whatever phase you wear, turn
upon our Roman brood, of old
      your shielding look.

35

Fetch, papyrus,
                    our soft-measured poet
our *confrère* Caecilius
                    down to Verona
fetch him down from the shores of Lake Como.
There are matters of moment a
mutual friend has to impart.
If you're wise you will swallow the miles
though a girl there calls back to you,
her blonde arms thrown round your neck
holding separation away . . .
who has been locked in desire
licked with the familiar flame
from the moment she first looked
at your new work – incomplete –
of the Great Mother
                    the destructive Queen.

You, madam,
                    a Sappho *de nos jours*
have Catullus's sympathy,
Caecilius has indeed sung his incomplete song
of Cybele
                    of her strong power over us all
with seduction.

36

Volusian sheets
shit-shotten Annals
discharge the pledge
that Lesbia makes
to Holy Venus
Holier Cupid:
– if I give
myself to her
alone, again,
discontinue
launching these
trucacious squibs,
on a pyre of
coffin chips she'll
burn the verses
of the meanest
Latin poet
read in Rome, a
votive blaze to
limping cuckolds. . . .
Thus with her
cerulean smile
has Lesbia pledged
a heavenly troth
in *trivia.* Hear,
Maid of sea-foam
Queen of Ancon
leafed Idalia
Cyprian Golgos
Amathusia

reed-bound Cnidos
Epidamnus
cross-roads of the
Adriatic,
take that vow as
here fulfilled and
neither lacking
wit nor point
in the performance:
burn script, blaze paper
into the fire you
rigmarole verse,
uncouth, banal
Volusian sheets,
shit-shotten Chronicle.

37

Nine posts, five doors, up the Clivus
  Victoriae, stands an
unsavoury resort . . . unsavoury
  habitués inside,
who think that only they have cocks,
  that only they can ruffle
a pudendum, the rest of us
  as apt as goats. I could
cheerfully bugger you all while
  you wait, kicking your heels.
Your numbers, a hundred or so,
  leave me undaunted. Think
of the man-power involved! And
  think of me now, scribbling
each of your names in black letters
  on the house-front. For she
whom once I loved as no other
  girl has been loved lives here.
Who has fled from my touch & sight.
  Whom I fought for & could
not keep. . . . A mixed bunch – successful,
  respectable men swap
places with dregs from the back-streets.
  She is open to all.
And one, who outdoes his home-grown
  rabbits – Egnatius,
the Spaniard with the beard, known for
  his wild dundrearies &
glistening teeth, assiduously
  (with native urine) scrubbed.

[95]

38

Angst,
      ennui & angst
consume my days & weeks,
and you have not written
or done anything to soothe my illness.
I am piqued.
      So much for our friendship.
Ah! Cornificius,
      a word from you would cure everything,
though more full of tears
      than a line from Simonides.

39

Because he has bright white teeth, Eg-
     natius whips out a
tooth-flash on all possible
     (& impossible) occasions.
You're in court. Counsel for defence
     concludes a moving per-
oration. (Grin.) At a funeral,
     on all sides heart-broken
mothers weep for only sons. (Grin.)
     Where, when, whatever the
place or time – grin. It could be a
     sort of 'tic'. If so, it's
a very *vulgar* tic, Egnatius,
     & one to be rid of.
A Roman, a Tiburtine or
     Sabine, washes his teeth.
Well-fed Umbrians & over-
     fed Etruscans wash theirs
daily. The dark Lanuvians
     (who don't need to), & we
Veronese, all wash our teeth. . . .
     But we keep them tucked in.
We spare ourselves the nadir of
     inanity – inane
laughter. You come from Spain. Spaniards
     use their morning urine
for tooth-wash. To us that blinding
     mouthful means one thing &
one only – the quantity of
     urine you have swallowed.

[97]

40

Whatever could have possessed you
to impale yourself on my iambics?
What ill-disposed deity inveigled you
Ravidus, into this one-sided contest?
Was it a letch for celebrity,
at no matter what cost?
                              – then you shall have it:
"Ravidus, loving in the place Catullus loves,
is lastingly nailed in this lampoon."

41

Formianus's whore,
                long-nosed
well-stuffed Ameana,
claims that I owe her
'a cool thousand' – for *services*!

Gather round, friends & relations
call in the medical practitioners
assemble your kinsfolk
and place the girl under analysis.
Why?
        She is clearly the victim of hallucinations
        (an advanced case of psychosis).

42

From the quarters of the compass
　　　gather round Catullus
indelicate syllables
　　　as many as you are,
a slippery whore has caught
　　　Catullus by the hairs.
She won't give me my pocket book back.
Come with Catullus
　　　follow her along the sidewalk
accost her on her beat
　　　insist she gives it back.
You ask, "Which one is yours?"
　　　The one parading in front
like a stage tart
　　　grinning like a French poodle.
Surround the little bitch
　　　insist she gives it back:
　　"My pocket book unwholesome whore
　　unwholesome whore my pocket book."
She looks the other way.
　　　"O tart of turpitude! O brothel lees!"
The brazen-faced bitch does not blush.
Approach again
　　　repeat in even louder tones:
　　"My pocket book unwholesome whore
　　unwholesome whore my pocket book."
We make no visible impression.
　　　The girl is totally unmoved.
Indelicate syllables
　　　to get our pocket book

we must adopt a change of front
        we must adopt new tactics
thus:
    "Intact young lady and of nubile rectitude
    would you be so kind as
    to give me back my pocket book?"

43

O elegant whore!
        with the remarkably long nose
unshapely feet
        lack lustre eyes
fat fingers
        wet mouth
and language not of the choicest,
you are I believe the mistress
of the hell-rake Formianus.

And the Province calls you beautiful;
they set you up beside my Lesbia.
O generation witless and uncouth!

44

It depends who's talking if you're a 'Sabine'
    or 'Tiburtine' grange: hurtful people lay odds
you're 'Sabine', to friends 'Tiburtine' – but one or
    t'other, Catullus scuttles happily
to shake off a bronchial chill in your sub-
    urban grove, stomach-earned from lunging after
grandiose food-dishes. Dinner with Sestius
    has meant reading his appalling speeches (the
Antian case): cold, vapid, unpleasant – I
    was at once affected, displayed signs of chill,
developed a phlegmatic wheeze and fled
    to your safety, where with rest & nettle broth
a cure has been effected. Refreshed, my thanks
    to you my grange, not rubbing in this *bêtise*.
Next time I finger that maleficent script
    let Sestius himself be seized with 'flu & phlegm,
who invites Catullus solely to make him read
    speeches so bad no one else will touch them.

45

Phyllis Corydon clutched to him
her head at rest beneath his chin.
He said, "If I don't love you more
than ever maid was loved before
I shall (if this the years not prove)
in Afric or the Indian grove
some green-eyed lion serve for food."
   Amor, to show that he was pleased,
   approvingly (in silence) sneezed.
Then Phyllis slightly raised her head
(her lips were full & wet & red)
to kiss the sweet eyes full of her:
"Corydon mine, with me prefer
a.ways to serve unique Amor:
my softer flesh the fire licks
more greedily and deeper sticks."
   Amor, to show that he was pleased,
   approvingly (in silence) sneezed.
So loving & loved so, they rove
between twin auspices of Love.
Corydon sets in his eye-lust
Phyllis before all other dust;
Phyllis on Corydon expends
her nubile toys, Love's dividends.
Could Venus yield more love-delight
than here she grants in Love's requite?

46

Now spring bursts
      with warm airs
now the *furor* of March skies
      retreats under Zephyrus . . .
and Catullus will forsake
      these Phrygian fields
the sun-drenched farm-lands of Nicaea
& make for the resorts of Asia Minor,
      the famous cities.
Now, the trepidation of departure
      now lust of travel,
feet impatiently urging him to be gone.
Good friends, good-bye,
      we, met in this distant place,
far from our Italy
      who by divergent paths
must find our separate ways home.

47

Lucius Calpurnius Piso Caesoninus
one circumcised Priapus of a proconsul
apparently prefers the company
      of a couple of society-mongers
Porcius & Socration
        his own mangy hirelings
to that of my dearest Veraniolus
my own dear Fabullus,
they dining well at the best places
you forced to hang about the street-corners
      angling for invitations.

48

Iuventius,
were I allowed
to kiss your eyes
as sweet as honey
on & on, three
thousand kisses
would not seem
too much for me,
as many as
ripe harvest ears
of sheaves of corn
would still not be
too much of kiss-
ing you, for me.

49

Silver-tongued among the sons of Rome
the dead, the living & the yet unborn,
Catullus, least of poets, sends
Marcus Tullius his warmest thanks:

– as much the least of poets
as he a prince of lawyers.

50

The other day we spent,
Calvus, at a loose end
flexing our poetics.
Delectable twin poets,
swapping verses, testing
form & cadence, fishing
for images in wine
& wit. I left you late,
came home still burning with
your brilliance, your invention.
Restless, I could not eat,
nor think of sleep. Under
my eyelids you appeared
& talked. I twitched, feverishly,
looked for morning . . . at last,
debilitated, limbs
awry across the bed
I made this poem of
my ardour & for our
gaiety, Calvus. . . . Don't
look peremptory, or
contemn my apple. Think.
The Goddess is ill-bred
exacts her hubris-meed:
lure not her venom.

51

Godlike the man who
sits at her side, who
watches and catches
　　　that laughter
which (softly) tears me
to tatters: nothing is
left of me, each time
　　　I see her,
... tongue numbed; arms, legs
melting, on fire; drum
drumming in ears; head-
　　　lights gone black.

Coda

Her ease is your sloth, Catullus
you itch & roll in her ease:

former kings and cities
lost in the valley of her arm.

52

Drop dead, Catullus, lie right down where you are & die.
That blister Nonnius occupies a magistrate's chair;
Vatinius commits perjury – & collects a consulate.
Drop dead, Catullus, just drop right down (& die).

53

I laughed. Calvus. I laughed today
when someone in the courtroom crowd, hearing
your quite brilliant *exposé* of
the Vatinian affair, lifted his hands up
in proper amazement, and cried suddenly:
"A cock that size . . . *and it spouts!*"
I laughed. Calvus. I laughed.

54

If not by all that his friends boast,
at least by pin-headed Otto's unattractive pate
by loutish Erius's half-washed legs
by Libo's smooth & judicious farts
by Sufficio's old man's lust turned green
may great Caesar be duly revolted. Once more
my naïve iambics strike home . . .

                                        unique general!

55

Where
      if it's not too much to ask
are you hiding,
      Camerius?
I've searched for you in the circus
in the parks
      among the bookstalls
even in Church (!)
      I have accosted
on Pompey's Broadway
      tart after tart,
meeting
      as you would expect
with a succession of blank looks.
"Where's Camerius, you low-down whores?"
One opens her bodice,
"You could find him between these pink tits
if you looked."
      A job,
I reflected, for Hercules.

      Why, Camerius
why arrogate to yourself this scarcity value? . . .

If I were Europa's bronze jailer
doing my rounds in Crete,
if I were fleet Ladas
      or feather-footed Perseus,
if I rode the sky like Pegasus
or with the dazzling swiftness of Rhesus' team,

– supposing I had the sandals of all the winds
I should still find myself sapped dry
eaten with fatigue
>   looking for you,
'friend'.
>   Come, Camerius, out with it
bare your precious secret to the day –
where are we likely to find you?
who are these girls
>   pliant as cream
who detain you?
>   Remember,
to keep the tongue locked in the mouth
is to reject love's seasoning:
love-talk enhances love-acts.
Alternatively,
>   if you want to,
bolt up your mouth . . .
>   only
divulge to Catullus the whereabouts of this *amour*,
>   so we may share her.

56

A matter for mirth, Cato, & a smile
worth your attention, you'll laugh
you'll laugh as you love your Catullus, Cato
listen – a matter for more than a smile!
Just now I found a young boy
      stuffing his girl,
I rose, naturally, and
      (with a nod to Venus)
fell and transfixed him there
with a good stiff prick,
        like his own.

57

Caesar Mamurraque!
A peerless pair of brazen buggers,
both tarred with the same brush
this, from the city
        that, from south Latium,
the stain ingrained no purgative can flush . . .
double dyed,
        the 'heavenly twins',
erudite in the skills of the one divan, each
as voraciously adulterous as the other –
joint competitors in the woman's market.
A peerless pair of brazen buggers!

58

Lesbia, our Lesbia, the same old Lesbia,
Caelius, she whom Catullus loved once
more than himself and more than all his own,
loiters at the cross-roads
                and in the backstreets
ready to toss-off the 'magnanimous' sons of Rome.

59

Menenius' wife,
           a red-headed cat from Bologna,
cat-like licks-off Rufulus. . . ,
You've seen her often
           in the public cemeteries,
scrounging for the food-offerings
           placed by the half-burnt bodies,
chasing the small loaves
           as they roll out of the fire,
and ducking a cuff
           from the unshaved corpse-heaver.

60

Hard. Hard. As she-cat whelped in desert mountains.
As Scylla's spawn spewed from the screaming vulvula.
As inhuman, precisely, as inflexible.
                              So, the supplication that
rises to you fresh as the new chance
– is scorned. Hard. Hard.

61

Hill (breeder) of Helicon,
        sun's seed of Urania,
        magnet a man is
for a maiden,
           Hymenaeus Hymen Io!
        Io! Hymen Hymenaeus.

Soft smell of marjoram
        melt on your forehead,
        cast the flame veil
come, joyfully:
        upon a white foot
               the saffron shoe.

Gaiety of daybreak!
           ringing voices
        shake out the bride-song!
        dance-throb in the fields,
tossing the pine torch,
        arms, waving.

Vinia comes to her altar,
        stands to her Manlius,
        shining as Venus to Paris,
rare fortune is born
        of a rare girl,

fair as the flowering Hamadryads
        or the myrtle they tend
        as their toy,

the shaft
shining,
wet with their dew:

Come, Hymen! come from your hill slopes
come from Aonian cave
from the Thespian rock
leave your cold nymph,
Aganippe,
– leave her her waters,

come! bring the bride home
set her, passionate,
beneath her new yoke
lock her up in her love
as the tree
fast in its ivy.

And you, girls innocent
of men,
whose own bride-day comes
come! shake out the bride-song:
'Hymenaeus Hymen Io!
Io! Hymen Hymenaeus.'

Happily cleaving the aether
the god's presence
descending
Hymen will answer your calls:
leading in Venus,
her bounties,
he couples true lovers.

[122]

Where else can the lover,
  tortured, turn?
   what greater god among men?
Hymenaeus Hymen Io!
  Io! Hymen Hymenaeus.

Trembling, the father
    hands you his daughter,
  for you, she'll unfasten
  her girl's girdle,
for your step, the bridegroom
  swollen with love, waits.

You pluck the flower
  from the mother's lap,
  in the novice's hand
the spray blossoms,
    Hymenaeus Hymen Io!
  Io! Hymen Hymenaeus.

There are no love-games,
  fairly played,
    without you,
  but with you
Venus luxuriates,
  where is your match among gods?

Absent, our homes
  are empty of children,
  parents barren of offspring,
with you –
  they proliferate!
  what greater god among gods?

[123]

Destitute of your sanctities
       the land is defenceless
       with you
she is inviolate,
        where is your match among gods?

Fling the doors wide
       she has come!
       See
         a shower
of torch flakes. . . .

    .   .   .   .

   .   .   .   .

       bashfully holds back,
       and steps
         hesitant
towards the threshold
       in tears –

no tears! Aurunculeia,
       the bright day will not see
       a more beautiful woman
than you
       spring from the sea:

a hyacinth of flowers,
       apart in a great garden,
       'a rich man's flower':
you linger: the day fades,
       shed your concealment!

[124]

Shed your concealment!
        a new bride
        hear our bride-speech,
see, the shower of torch flakes!
        shed your concealment!

No fickle lusts,
        no rooting between
        other sheets –
your husband will lie
        only in the valley of your breasts,

a 'hero' caught in your arms
        as the grape pole
        caught in the twisting vine.
See! the day fades:
        shed your concealment!

O bed in which all. . . .
  .   .   .   .
  .   .   .   .
  .   .   .   .
        and at the white foot of the bed.

Venus will shine for him
        in the vague night,
        blaze
        at mid-day.
The day fades:
        new bride, shed your concealment!

Toss the pine torches!
        see, the flame

veil approaching,
shake out the bride-song!
Hymenaeus Hymen Io!
Io! Hymen Hymenaeus.

Ribaldry of marriage
and nuts
nuts
for the scrambling boys,
friend!
that sort of love is finished,

a cascade of nuts!
listless you may be:
you've played with nuts
in your time
now Talasius waits on your service,
a cascade of nuts!

No servant girl to his taste
or to yours
until now
(and the barber scrapes your first hairs)
come,
a cascade of nuts!

Does the 'well dressed groom'
letch
after former smooth cheeks?
– *that* sort of love is over,
Hymenaeus Hymen Io!
Io! Hymen Hymenaeus.

[126]

Yours were the licensed joys,
    but the licence
          expires
with your marriage,
Hymenaeus Hymen Io!
    Io! Hymen Hymenaeus.

And Lavinia, let your man ride
    how he will – where he will,
    or you'll find him riding elsewhere,
Hymenaeus Hymen Io!
    Io! Hymen Hymenaeus.

The *châtelaine*
    of a fine house,
    dispenser of influence,
Hymenaeus Hymen Io!
    Io! Hymen Hymenaeus,

until, white with woman's age
    the old head
    quivers all day
in endless assent,
        Hymenaeus Hymen Io!
    Io! Hymen Hymenaeus.

Now, in the saffron shoe,
          with fair omens,
    step over the threshold
    approach the porch doors,
Hymenaeus Hymen Io!
    Io! Hymen Hymenaeus.

[127]

Within, stretched on the Tyrian couch
                your one man
                swelling with love
waits for you only,
                        Hymenaeus Hymen Io!
                Io! Hymen Hymenaeus.

A withering flame
                stirs in him
                        as in you,
                but his the deeper,
less radiant, heat,
                        Hymenaeus Hymen Io!
                Io! Hymen Hymenaeus.

Page, let go
                the bride's arm
                let her come
to her bride-bed,
                        Hymenaeus Hymen Io!
                Io! Hymen Hymenaeus,

and you women,
                practised in bride-bed
                and birth-bed
                        disarray her
bring her to Hymen,
                        Hymenaeus Hymen Io!
                Io! Hymen Hymenaeus.

Now Manlius stands at the bed
                where she waits

shining
a lily among yellow field-flowers:
she lies,
white on the saffron sheets.

But Manlius has
his own love-gifts
Venus has blessed him:
come, do not linger –
the day fades,

and he comes, straight to the bedhead,
with Venus inside him
he takes his desire
in full view:
love knows no concealments.

Assessing their love is like counting
the stars in the sky
or the sands
in the African desert:
theirs are a hundred love games.

Play out your love games
freely and swiftly
plant the new shoot
an old name cannot lapse
you must make, in the one place,
constant renewal.

May a diminutive Torquatus
drop from Lavinia's womb

[129]

waving pink arms
with a smile (first)
            for his father,

whose stamp he must carry
            plain to the world,
            the bond
of his mother's
            fidelity,

and Lavinia will rank
            with Penelope,
            chaste in the birth
of Telemachus:
            archetype of wives.

Fold the doors softly,
            bridesmaids,
            feasting is over,
let them ply arms and legs
                        in their love-games,
            the constant renewal.

62

Young Men

Gather young men as the twilight gathers
      Vesper gleams faintly in heaven
it is time to bestir
      time to abandon the wedding tables
for the bride comes through the dusk
      it is time for the bride-hymn.
    Hymen Hymenaeus attend O Hymen!

Maidens

Watch where the young men gather by the porch-doors
face them while Vesper hangs fire over Thessaly
they are gathering quickly
      intent on their song
on contesting the bride-song with us
      response versus response.
    Hymen Hymenaeus attend O Hymen!

Young Men

Here is no palm for the asking
      observe these
young girls conferring together with girlish seriousness,
their care
      a sole-minded intensity
must
      produce the worth while,
while we
      distracted
deserve our defeat
      our minds on the one thing

with only an ear for the song:
   success waits on devotion.
Come! bend minds to the business
   girls flower in song
   man makes response.
  Hymen Hymenaeus attend O Hymen!

Maidens

What flame glows more pitilessly in heaven than yours
Vesper:
   under your gaze
the daughter wrenched from her mother's clasp,
   from the mother's clasp
twined there
   torn apart
her maidenhead placed under a young man's burning hand:
what jackbooting of lost cities
   pitiless as such an act?
  Hymen Hymenaeus attend O Hymen!

Young Men

What flame shines more resplendently in heaven than yours
Vesper:
   under your sign the marriage bond is sealed
the young man's troth
   the father's pledge
is effected
   in your ardour the consummation is joined:
what hour from the gods
   resplendent as such an hour?
  Hymen Hymenaeus attend O Hymen!

Maidens

Vesper has bereft us of one. . . .

.   .   .   .   .

Young Men

With your rising
            the night watchman guards against
furtive lovers on the prowl by night
            whom you as Lucifer
may disconcertingly discover
            still at their thefts
for maidens' acts belie their mock complaints,
affecting aversion
            for what they most desire.
            Hymen Hymenaeus attend O Hymen!

Maidens

When withdrawn in some walled garden
            a rose blooms
safe from the farm plough
            from farm beasts
strong under sun
            fresh in light free air
sprouting in rain showers
that rose is beauty's paragon for man or woman's pleasure,
but once the bud has blown
            – when the thin stalk is left
no paragon remains for man or woman's pleasure:
so, intact
            a girl stays treasured of her sex
but let her lose her maidenhead
            her close petals once polluted

she cannot give the same delight again to men
no longer be the cynosure of virgins.
Hymen Hymenaeus attend O Hymen!

Young Men

When in an open field
unyoked a vine droops
no vine-limbs shake to the wind
no ripe grape-clusters sprout
there the soft plant stoops under its own weight
the vine-tips flop to their roots
that vine no hind nor husbandman will husband,
but yoke her to her elm-pole mate
and hinds & husbandmen in droves will husband her:
so, intact
a girl grows withered in her sex
but yoke her to her mate in her ripe season
she will yield her parents ease
she will yield delight to men.
Hymen Hymenaeus attend O Hymen!

Young Men & Maidens

Resign as your father resigns you to this man
strength lies in surrender
father & mother in concert
resign you,
incline to their will
remember your
own maidenhead is not truly your own
one part to your father
one to your mother
only a third to yourself

[134]

incline then to their will & consign
    your share as they theirs
with the bride-gift,
    to this man
    in wedlock.
    Hymen Hymenaeus attend O Hymen!

63

Plunging towards Phrygia over violent water
shot on the wood-slung Berecynthian coast
Attis with urgent feet treads the opaque ground
of the Goddess, his wits fuddled, stung with phrenetic
itch, slices his testicles off with a razor-
flint, sees the signs of new blood spotting
the earth, knows arms, legs, torse, sans
male members and
                    SHE
ecstatically snatches in delicate hands
the hand-drum of Cybebe, the hand-drum
of forest rites and Cybebe's torture
with nervous fingers taps the hollowed hide
shakes it and shaking summons the Mother's Brood:
"Ololugmos!
            To Cybebe's thickets!
                            You have found the strange coast.
Ololugmos!
        Stamp in my footprints!
                            You are tied to my tether.
Ololugmos!
        Capsized in my currents –
                            unsexing yourselves
in my Love-hate.
            Ololugmos! Break the close thicket,
with rabid abandon brighten Dindymia's face
stamp on Cybebe's ground
                    stamp where the drum shudders
stamp where the cymbals clang
                    where the flute drones

[136]

where the Maenads convulsively toss their ivied heads
where the protracted scream signals the Maenad rite –
the carlines flit restlessly in the grove
– Come with your quick triple step,
                                    Ololugmos!"
As Attis speaks
              the trembling tongues of her neophytes
rise with the drum beats,
                            the concave cymbals begin clanging.
They head for green Ida.
                        Attis is a frenzied steer.
She gasps
        goaded by yoke-hate
bursts through the holy grove,
                              the throbbing drums
the foot-mad Gallae, stream in her wake. . . .
And the touch of Cybebe's bower brings lassitude.
Fatigue lowers their lids. They are foodless.
Investing apathy unstrings the manic pitch.
They sleep.
            Then when the sun's manifold hooves splinter
darkness, and the eyes from the gold mask sweep sky &
  earth
& the wild sea, Sleep takes a nimble dive from waking Attis into the expectant arms of his paramour
                                          – Pasithea.
At once, shedding the night's tranquillity, Attis
relives the pictures in her heart,
                                  freed from the maelstrom,
unclouded, recognises the rootless place where she has
  come,
her thoughts turned inside out, goes headlong back

[137]

to the beach, where she cries to Attica she has lost
for ever . . . looks over the brutal water
that stares back at her through her tears:
"Attica mother & maker, I
like a grateless housecarl fleeing
his mesne, footloose among Ida's
snows among the wood & rock lairs
with the boar caves for an icy hearth,
have I stripped myself of my patrimony
friends, goods, kin?

                  Are these ungreek landscapes
my new life-home?

                Where is Attica?
Where can the pupil open with Attica?
The storm has lifted

              and there is no *piazza*,
where is the stadium? the wrestling ring? the gymnasium
– a fallen life left to tread sorrow.
What have I not known? What shape not been?
A synthetic woman:

                 once man, once lad, once boy.
Once the flower of the athletes.

                Once the pride of the young wrestlers.
My doors & thresholds were warm with friends.
The house full of blossoms greeting
the morning separation from the lover's couch.
And now, I, but part 'I',

               a plucked torse
a Maenad

     familiar of the gods

              huscarl of Cybebe,
tethered under these obsessive peaks

rooting with the tree-stag & the boar
                   in the snow woods,
the pain at Attis' heart outweighs the Attis rage."
As the words fly from the pink mouth
they lodge in Cybebe's ears
who stoops to the fear-of-flocks
unyokes the left-hand lion
and whispers:
              "Attis is truant. Hound Attis hither.
Infect her with fear & desire
for Cybebe's pale. Lash at yourself with
your tail-knot. Drown the whole mountain
with roaring. Let the red mane dreadfully
cloud the brute neck."
                  She looses the leash.
The beast self-scourges its flanks
bounds through the brushwood, bursts
on the white-lined sands, appearing
where delicate Attis still stands by the sea.
The demented creature flees to Cybebe's wold
her life-space doomed spent in Cybebe's thrall.

"Great Cybebe, Mother Goddess, Berecynthian Queen,
avert your fury from Catullus' house
goad others to your actions,
others trap in the snarl of frenzy."

64

In old days
                    driving through soft waters
to the River of Pheasants
                    to the end of the Euxine Lake
pines sprung from Pelion
                    carrying picked men
Argives each like a tree
                    hearts set on the Colchian pelt
of gold, daring to track
                    salt deserts in a fast ship
cutting blue waves with firwood blades
for whom the indweller of the arx
                    the queen of hill-castles
had made hull poop & sail
                    – volatile under light winds –
binding firmly the pine-plaits to the curved underprow
the first boat to experience innocent sea –
Amphitrite.
                    As the moving waves took the keel
the water, chopped with oars, grew white
and from the runnels of foam faces peered
of Nereids, wondering. Then
and not since
                    men with their own eyes
saw the bare bodies of nymphs
                    in broad daylight
caught in the marbled runnels of foam
as far down as the nipples. . . .
So Peleus was stirred towards Thetis
so Thetis came to a woman's bridal

and Jove gave his blessing.
                         O heroes
brides nymphs oreads
                 born in a golden time
before the tribe of gods had gone from earth
I call on you in my poem
                 standing with Peleus
Pillar of Thessaly
                 blest beyond most in their bride-torches
whom Jove himself
                 author of gods and goddesses
has given one of his girls,
                 and Thetis
prettiest of mermaids
                 touched as her own,
whom Tethys & old Ocean
                 girdling all that we stand on –
have yielded a granddaughter.
                 On the day
the longed-for light leaps up
Thessaly gathers in concourse
                 gift-bearing guests
a laughing crowd
                 their hearts in their faces
converge on the Palace.
                 Cieros is empty
Phthiotic Tempe deserted
                 the houses in Crannon
Larissa's walls
                 abandoned –
flocking into Pharsalia
                 packed under Pharsalian roofs

[141]

the crowds gather.
              No man tills the field
the bullock's neck grows soft.
              Not for many days shall the pronged hoe
rake among the vine-roots,
              or the pruning hook lessen
the olive tree's deep shade.
              Oxen do not turn the lumps of loam,
              red rust flakes the neglected plough.
But in the royal halls
              wherever you look
as room unfolds into room
              silver & gold gleam
an effulgence of ivory,
              carved thrones,
glittering cups on the long tables
the whole building thrums with the splendour of royal
   goods,
and there, in the middle,
              inlaid with Indian tooth
and quilted with arras,
              the divan of the small goddess
              the arras ochred with rock-lichen &
              tinctured with stain of rose shell-fish.

This quilt is pricked
              with figures of gods & men
sketches of antiquity in *petit point*!
Here are the never-silent sands of Naxos
here Theseus vanishes towards the north,

a woman watches from the empty beach
                unflagging grief in her heart,
Ariadne doesn't yet believe, quite,
                she is witnessing what her eyes see –
she's only just woken from a trap
(of sleep)
        found herself alone on the island.
And Theseus, heedless as storm & wind
                carves up the waves as he goes
and throws their love-words overboard.
                But the Minoan girl
with seaweed on her legs
                goes on looking from the shallow water
with tragic eyes
                she goes on looking from a long way
frozen in the statuary of grief,
                like a Maenad,
until waves of her own shake her
                her hair shakes loose of her yellow snood
her thin bodice flaps open at her breasts
her breasts, the colour of milk,
                push through her torn brassiere,
snood skirt bra
                the shallows take her torn clothes
swirling the silk in eddies at her ankles
the clothes do not matter:
                her body is lost in you
Theseus –
                Ariadne!
Venus has kept for you her best thorn of love
love-fated girl
                love-fated from the hour Theseus

[143]

steered from the curved breakwater of the Piraeus
set course for the iron city of the iron king
Minoan Knossos.

        A blight lay over the narrow streets of Athens. . .
The story goes that to absolve herself
of the murder of the bull-king's son
                   Androgeos
at the games at the Panathenaea
        Athens yielded
yearly ten of her best men
yearly ten nubile girls (unmarried)
        food for the bull-king
until Prince Theseus one day
        proffered himself for his sweet city,
"The shipments of the dead not dead
from here to Crete shall stop".
He sailed in a good ship, before fine winds,
coming to the rock-hewn halls of Knossos.
From her window
        the royal girl looked down
with a girl's lust,
        whom the women's quarters enfolded
in her chaste bed
        as petals the scented stamen
who was like the myrtle buds on the banks of the Eurotas
or the coloured breath of springtime
not lifting her hot eyes
           till fire ran in her womb –
        the girl's body swathed in fire.
Remorseless Cupid

Holy Child
      – who stirs hate & love in one cup!
Venus of Eryx
      – a girl who will drown in your floods
      whispering at a blond stranger!
Venus of Golgos
      – and expectations breaking in the heart!
Venus of leafy Idalia
      – how often the girl's cheeks – sallow, like gold!
As Theseus walked out to meet the beast
poised between death and celebrity
Ariadne addressed herself to her prayers
                    with firm lips
making her small offerings to the gods,
who acted.
      For as on the top of Mount Taurus
in Turkey
      where the great oaks shake out their boughs
and the pine trees drip resin
      a high wind contorting the trunk
can pluck out a tree by its roots
      so that the monster upended
comes down beamwise
      splintering what's in its path
so Theseus capsized the bull-monster
      and the quelled body lay in a heap
its fruitless horns sticking up.
      Then fingering the thread
he turned his feet back,
      along the delusive maze
of palace corridors,
      stepped out of the labyrinth

[145]

a hero, unharmed
                and made off with the girl
– prizing sweet love & Theseus
                before the lot of them
eluding her father's watch
forgoing her three sisters' embraces
                                        her mother's,
tearful for a lost daughter
whom the wind blew to white-ringed Naxos
whom sleep took in the night
whom yesterday's bridegroom
                                forsworn
left, before morning.

                And now scared at her own grief
scattering her screams broadside
                she runs to the top of the cliffs
looks at the waves rolling northwards
then runs out into the sea
                holding her silk petticoat above her knees,
glass-cheeked,
        at the end of tears,
        and frozen with tears,
the words well from the pit of her bride's stomach:

"Why did you lift me from Cretan bower
"dumping me here on an empty beach,
"shrugging off Heaven, her plans for us,
"heedless of freighting home snapped pledges?
"Nowhere the means to flex steel

"no appeal that could touch you.
"You did not tell me to look for seduction
"but for bride-ale & wedding torches,
"for the increments of Hymen,
"– waste words shredded now on wind.
"Now no woman listen to man's love-words
"or look to find there his love-bond:
"as long as they itch for it
"they will say anything
                    do anything,
"but with lust slaked
            "the soft words are forgotten
            "the promises null.
"I caught you from the back coil of your fate
"happy to exchange a half-brother for love's need
"and you leave me – scavenge for island birds & beasts:
            "no tumulus for me dead
            "no death-dust as cover.
"You are flint
            where the bitch-cat whelps under desert rock,
"or spume
        when brine-water sickens with sea-spawn,
"you are the kindless issue of the twin gulfs
                            – storm-ridden Syrtes –
"of the octopus & the maelstrom,
                        epitomes of ruin.
"Is this your guerdon for a life saved?
"If you did not want to marry me
"because of your father (who is prejudiced)
"you could have taken me home with you
"and I should have tended you
"got your bath ready for you,

[147]

"washing your arms & feet with spring water,
"each day smoothing the coloured bedspread in your
  room.
"But why should I give my tears
"to this wind? In this state?
"Wind is deaf as well as dumb.
"And he's wind-driven in the middle distance.
"There's nothing here but rocks & seaweed.
"In the hubris of indifference Fate
"deprives me even of an ear to listen.
"If only the Athenian sloop
"had never entered the bay
"at Knossos, with its grim cargo
"for the bull, fixed hawsers to the quay,
"captained by an attractive sailor . . .
"with a soul like a trap-door
"whom we took in out of pity –

              his name was Theseus.

"Where can I go?

         What is left for me?

"Our Cretan hills?

         There's bitter water between.

"A father?

      Whom I abandoned in blood guilt.

"Or the love-purpose of a husband?
"Who makes the rowlocks creak
"in his hurry to get away from me.
"And inland on Naxos?

            Derelict

"no roof-tree

      no escape

"the surcingle of sea-water

"no hope
          no reason for refuge
"all is dumb
          all is alone
                    all is nothing
"but these lids won't grow grubby with death
"till from the gods I've wrung amercement –
"on Olympus someone tips back the scales.
"Listen:
          raveners of men's evil
                              Erinyes
"upon whose scalps
               as images of hate
"snakes feed,
          Tisiphone!
                    Megaera!
"Alecto!
          these moans are forced
"from a feverish body,
"as blind as epilepsy,
"they are the truth of Ariadne's heart.
"Don't waste what galls,
"make Theseus deal
"as brutally as he dealt me
"himself & someone loved."

As the voice poured from the tragic mouth
crying for revenge on the ill dealt her
Jove's brow bent in assent
so that land and wild sea shook,
the gleaming stars shivered in the sky

[149]

and a mist fell on Theseus
who at once forgot the strict words,
till then locked in his heart,
that he signal careworn Aegeus
by hoisting the glad-omened sails
when the home port hove in sight.
For before Theseus slipped anchor
dropping beneath the city's ramparts
his father had kissed him
yielding his son to sea-winds
with the words:

"Restored at the tail-end of my life
"from Troezene, my only Theseus
"dearer than years to your father
"of whom Fate & your own zest
"would rob him a second time,
"even before his failing eyes
"had gotten used to your face,
"I despatch you without happiness
"banning bravado of flags & auguries.
"I make public grief
"with dust & ash on my grey hair
"and the dark canvas hung
"from your voyaging mast:
"Hibernian dyed purple
"signal of foreboding.
                But should Athene
"shield of Athens & of Athenians
"stoop to sprinkle your right hand
"with the bull's blood, enact closely

"heart-kept, unflecked by time
"this mandate:
                    On sight of Attic hills
"to strip ship of purple
"& hoist white sails from the plaited cords
"so Aegeus, at the first, may see
"with carefree heart his son safe,
"Theseus bent homeward in bright-omened hour."

But these words locked in intention
drifted from Theseus' head
as the wind imperceptibly lifts
the snow-mist from the hill-tops.
For Aegeus posted himself in the watch-tower,
his eyes tear-gutted,
he saw the dark shrouds
he read the false news of death
and the old king cast himself from the battlements,
while the boy, fresh from the bull-killing
'came home' – entered a stricken palace
victim of deceit as grim
as he off Naxos coast had sprung
bewildered Ariadne –

        . . . who still gazes where the hull has dwindled,
who revolves in her bride's heart a maze of sorrow.

                    And elsewhere on the quilt
flushed with desire for the Minoan bride

[151]

Bacchus his crew
of Satyrs & Silenes
            descend about the glittering god,
from Ethiopia, from Ind, from Thrace
            with tossing heads
with frenzied 'Evoes!'
            they are shaking the thyrsus
shaking the vine leaves round it,
            they catch the torn bits of bullock
the snake belt writhes at their hips
            and the secret *cartouche*
hiding the sacred objects
            objects no common sight profanes
passes to the hand-slap drum beat,
            bagpipe, horn & cymbals
sprinkle the hillside with discordant music.

Such the stitches worked in the wedding quilt,
such the splendid figures embracing the divan.
The young guests from Thessaly
their eyes filled with the tapestry
gradually ebb
            from courts & corridors,
the demi-gods are due:
            it is a dawn figure,
Aurora climbs
            to the threshold of the day-sojourning sun,
Zephyr
            flicks the flat water into ridges
with a morning puff,
            the sloped waves

[152]

loiter musically,
　　　　later the wind rises
& they rise,
　　　　they multiply,
they shed the sun's sea purple as they flee.
In this way
　　　　the crowd scatters from the royal crannies,
the mortal guests disperse to their own homes.

And now, Chiron,
　　　　first to arrive,
carrying from Mount Pelion
　　　　green gifts
of Thessalian buds
　　　　from fields & alps
from river banks
　　　　where the light west wind
has unsealed them.
　　　　It is the centaur's *potpourri*.
They luxuriate
　　　　through the wedding rooms
with a confused fragrance.
　　　　And behind Chiron,
Peneus
　　　　bearded with rushes
from Tempe
　　　　whose girdling woods
are a river roof.
　　　　He brings
store of beech
　　　　dripping roots,

[153]

& laurel
        like a girl's flanks,
he brings the plane tree
        that is restless,
the piercing cypress
        & the poplar
supple in the wind,
        its tears of amber
for flame-shrouded Phaeton.
        The river god
heaps the foliage
        outside & in
until the house
        is dressed
for a bride's bower-bed.
        Next, Prometheus
patron of crafts
        & seer
still showing
        the faint cicatrices
Jove's penance
        paid on the cliff-face
in Caucasus,
        rock-chained
arms & legs
        thirty years. . . .
And then follows Jove,
        Juno,
their issue –
        only Apollo
the archer
        & his twin sister, Artemis,

[154]

have spurned
        the bride-ale & wedding torches
and are left to haunt Heaven.

The gods have disposed
        their white forms
at the wedding tables.
        It is bride-hymn time.
The Parcae prepare
        to intone
the prophetic song.
        The white shift
wrapping their palsy
        is alive,
it is red-hemmed
        at the ankles,
and their white hair
        is bound
with a red cloth.
        Their deft fingers
manipulate
        the eternal thread,
one hand on the distaff
        the other carding
with upturned fingers
        the spindle wool,
drawing the thread
        downwards,
twirling the whorl
        as the thread lengthens,

and stooping
  with mauve lips
to bite the rough ends off
  so that the bits hang
from the withered skin.
  An osier basket bulges
with new-shorn fleece . . .
  the wool whirrs
and the clear voices ring
  in Epithalamion
for Thetis,
  her bride-doom
time-sealed.

"Emathian bulwark, son of Jove,
whose acts augment his born worth,
accept the sisters' wedding truth.

Inexorably, fate follows thread,
from spindle to the shuttle running.

Fair-fortuned star that draws the bride
to groom, that yields the longed-for wife
whose mastery of love will drown
his heart, who settling to the drawn-
out marriage sleep will make her arms
light cushions for his heavy neck.

Inexorably, fate follows thread,
from spindle to the shuttle running.

[156]

Not yet such love as Peleus
for Thetis holds (& she for him)
has been – or such a grove of love.

Inexorably, fate follows thread,
from spindle to the shuttle running.

A child, Achilles, void of fear:
foe known face-on not fleeing, first
in racing, in hunt fleeter than
the fleet-foot stag, whose hooves strike flame.

Inexorably, fate follows thread,
from spindle to the shuttle running.

No warrior dare confront Achilles
where the Trojan rivers stream with
Trojan blood, and the Greeks raze stone
from stone of Troy, ten years consumed.

Inexorably, fate follows thread,
from spindle to the shuttle running.

The women at the gravesides weep
his deeds, their hair is loose, coated
with ash-dust, their ageing bosoms
showing fist marks of their sorrow.

Inexorably, fate follows thread,
from spindle to the shuttle running.

[157]

As the farmer's scythe in close-packed
cornstalks, stripping the yellow field,
his fierce blade crops Troy's men-at-arms.

Inexorably, fate follows thread,
from spindle to the shuttle running.

Scamander by quick Hellespont
will watch his valour swell, its width
shrink with slaughter-stooks, while its deep
course warms with the issuing blood.

Inexorably, fate follows thread,
from spindle to the shuttle running.

And Polyxena, death-given,
too shall watch . . . and watch the earth-tomb
rise, where her maiden limbs will fall.

Inexorably, fate follows thread,
from spindle to the shuttle running.

Once Chance lets slip the Greeks inside
the sea-born belt of stone, the young
girl's blood will soak the barrow mound,
who crouches to the two-edged sword
& pitches, a headless trunk, forward.

Inexorably, fate follows thread,
from spindle to the shuttle running.

[158]

But now the joining of their loves,
as Peleus accepts his nymph, &
Thetis lightly yields to wedlock.

Inexorably, fate follows thread,
from spindle to the shuttle running.

And dawn light finds the nurse who tries
today's neck fillet, her mother reads
the sign & smiles: the goddess was
not coy in love – young fruit will follow.

Inexorably, fate follows thread,
from spindle to the shuttle running."

This song
        of happy wedding-fates
the Parcae sang
        to Peleus
in old days.
        For once
when piety had place on earth
        the gods themselves
stood at our chaste doors
        or drank at the bride-ales
of mortal heroes.
        On Holy Feasts
Jove from his bright throne
saw the earth littered with a hundred bulls.
The wine-god on Parnassus
        goading his dishevelled troop

[159]

was hailed
      with altar smoke
from happy Delphos
      where the rasping Thyiades
had emptied street & square.
      Athene, Mars or Artemis
appeared
      in the death-tussle
and lit men's hearts.
      To-day ill wreaking rules.
Man's piety is fled.
      The loveless child neglects its parent's death
      a brother's blood trickles from brothers' hands
      the first son's girl attracts the father's lust
      who seeks a step-dame & a son's demise
      unwittingly the youngster mounts his mother
      her vicious incest spurning the house-kin
      spirits: laws bouleversé, and the welter
      such, those of Hill-Heaven have withdrawn their care.

No longer do they deign
to keep our bride-ales, or
reveal themselves to us
in the light of common day.

65

Although entangled in prolonged grief
severed from the company of the Muses
and far from Pieria
      my brain children still-born
myself among Stygian eddies
the eddies plucking at the pallid foot
of a brother
      who lies under Dardanian soil
stretched by the coastland
      whom none may now hear
none touch
      shuttered from sight
whom I treasured more than this life
and shall –
      in elegies of loss
plaintive as Procne crying under the shadow of the
  cypress
for lost Itylus,
      I send, Hortalus, mixed with misery
Berenice's Lock –
      clipped from Callimachus
for you might think my promise
had slipped like vague wind through my head
or was like the apple
      unavowed
the girl takes from her lover
      thrusts into her soft bodice
and forgets there . . .
      till her mother takes her off guard –
she is startled,

[161]

the love-fruit trundles ponderously across the
floor
and the girl, blushing, stoops gingerly
to pick it up.

66

Who scans the bright machinery of the skies
& plots the hours of star-set & star-rise,
this or that planet as it earthward dips,
the coursing brightness of the sun's eclipse,
who knows the dreams that fill Endymion's head
& draw sly Cynthia to his Latmian bed –
palace astronomer, whose gaze is set
more earnestly on Heaven than on *Debrett*,
by you this soft effulgence first was seen
who knew at once the ringlets of the Queen,
those ringlets Berenice with bridal care
pledged when the King left for the Syrian war
(the suppliant Queen with tender arms outspread
the King still swollen from the marriage bed),
who carries with him marks of sweeter strife,
the night's clear traces of a virgin wife!
      Are brides averse to Venus (as they show)
or are their tears transparencies of woe
brilliantly shed amidst the wedding scene
effective bar to *you know what I mean?*
Their tears are false. I saw a bride's tears shed
when wartime took her husband from her bed.
Still wedded to the Queen's resplendent hair
I witnessed Berenice's crude despair.
And does she wail a so-called 'brother' gone,
or that she lies in bed at night alone,
her body wasted with intensive fire,
her soul devoid of all save one desire?
The proof is here, for virgin she displayed
a spirit commoner in man than maid.

When her betrothed preferred her mother's charms
she saw him slain, couched in Apáme's arms,
procuring by such resolute despatch
her present Kingdom (with a King to match).
Then why this gale of wife-forsaken sighs,
the trembling tears brushed from the brimming eyes?
What God is this, unless the God of Love,
who cannot brook his servants' long remove?
For Ptolemy, all Egypt's altars smoke
and hecatombs of bullocks loose their yoke,
while I, a ransom from a loving head,
secure a husband's swift return to bed,
who conquers Syria, the Euphrates crosses,
views India & returns with trifling losses.
Whisked hence by Venus, lo! these few hairs set
in starry payment of the royal debt.

      And yet with grief, O Queen, I left your hair,
a grief attested by your own coiffure,
by which I vow (& none vows there in vain)
no hair exists that scissors can't obtain.
Scissors & hair? Before the touch of steel
the tallest mountains have been known to reel.
Athos itself, the Guardian of the Coast,
bent to the pickaxe of the Persian host,
whereat the Thian forbears of your crown
watched a fleet passing & a mountain drown.
For women's locks what help, when such as these
yield to the metal of the Chalybes?
A plague on smithies, be they crude or fine,
cursed be the smelter, cursed the teeming mine!

      My loss was freshly mourned, when Venus sent
black Memnon's brother with Divine intent.

[164]

The winged familiar mounts; he fans the air;
he bears me upwards through the darkening sphere
until in Heaven he lays me safe at rest
in the chaste dove-cote of Cytherea's breast.
Translated thus, at Queen Arsínoe's word,
I join (though wet with tears) the golden horde.
No more shall Ariadne's Crown alone
gleam from the threshold of the Heavenly Throne:
these holy spoils (with hers) must share from now
th' immortal honours of a mortal brow.
The older stars make room. The Gods declare.
th' apotheosis of a lock of hair.

     Shielding the Virgin from the Lion's wrath,
(below the Bear that glisters in the North)
trampled by night upon the Milky Way ·
to kindly Tethys then restored by day,
westward I wheel, leading slow Boötes on
loth to sink seawards e'er the night has gone.
Unlooked-for Fate! 'Tis ill to tempt the Maid –
more abject still to leave the Truth unsaid,
or, fearful of a God's offended smart,
forbear to lend expression to the heart.
Know: less a source of gladness than of sighs
my elevation to the brilliant skies,
my heavenly lustres shine (to me) less clear
than those that hung from Berenice's ear,
who used to smooth me with sweet oils & scent
though not with myrrh, nor married ornament.

     Pour then for me, upon your bridal night,
before you doff your silks & quench the light,
before your eager bosom you yield up,
the mingled fragrance of the onyx cup,

onyx, whose contents have so often led
to the chaste dalliance of the marriage bed.
Let the false tokens of unwedded lust
degraded sink into the wasteful dust.
Favoured the bride whose offerings I accept,
her husband constant, she in love adept.

      When, Berenice, you come to Venus' rites
amid the cerem'ny of palace lights,
when gazing upwards (in the cause of Love),
you fix your eyes upon the stars above,
recall the 'simple' scents I knew in life
& pour the perfumes proper to a wife.

      Let but Aquarius with Orion shine,
the stars fall inward and this Lock Divine
be placed once more on that fair head of thine!

67

Catullus

Sweet entrance to a husband's pleasure
        door Jove cram with goodness!
pleasant too for grandpapa's lust
        door that worked well for Balbus
while the old man was alive
        then switched fealty to madam
shutting yourself on the *ci-devant*
        face: decay possessed the old
one: they laid him out stiff & bare.
Whence this *volte-face* from husband to young wife?

Door

This, Quintus, a whitewashed door,
        is currently fee-held
of Caecilius. Envious
        onlookers indeed would
make me their whipping post & say,
"Door you are the port-hole to filthy vice".

Catullus

Your words are unconvincing: deeds
        bring words to sight & touch.

Door

How show this? Who cares?

Catullus

        Catullus.
Unlock yourself to him.

Door

Then listen. The virgin lifted
                across this threshold was
bogus, the groom not the first to
                finger her, and his short
sword hung like a strip of limp beet
                between his legs, never
cocked navelwards. And worse. Grandpa
                defiled his own son's sheets
polluting the fallen house, either
                from his own incest-blaze
or from his son's nerveless testicles.
                A steadier hand was needed
satisfactorily to unfasten . . .
to undo properly, her suspender belt.

Catullus

Egregious parent to ejac-
ulate in his son's private vulvula!

Door

There is more out of Brescia,
                overhung by Cycnean
cliffs, inthreaded by the honey-
                watered Mella, mother
of your loved Verona: there is
                gossip of an affair –
Postumius & Cornelius &
                her ill-sex with the two.

[168]

Catullus

There are people to question a
        door's knowledge of such things:
one who cannot leave the house to
        eavesdrop in the market
or step far from this lintel, swing-
        ing in & out all day.

Door

I have often caught her whispers
        with her maids rehearsing
their love-parties. I am sans ears
        sans tongue. They laugh. The same
names crop up, & a long red man's,
        whose name I bar from respect
of a disapproving eyebrow:
        there was trouble there when
he claimed cash from the family in
        respect of a reputed
impregnation of the daughter's lying belly.

68

Borne down by bitter misfortune
you send me this letter, Manlius,
blotted with tears,
       it comes like flotsam
from a spumy sea –
       from the shipwreck of your affairs –
a cry from the undertow . . .
and that you,
       whom Venus deprives
of soft sleep,
       whom the Greek Muse
no longer tempts,
       who turn restlessly
in an empty bed,
       call me 'my friend',
that you look to Catullus
       for love-gifts of Venus
& of the Holy Muses,
       is a gift in itself,
but your own tears blind you to mine.
I am not neglectful of friendship,
but we two squat in the same coracle,
we are both swamped by the same stormy waters,
I have not the gifts of a happy man. . . .
Often enough,
       when a man's toga first sat on my shoulders
I chased love & the Muses,
       in the onset of youth
the tart mixture of Venus
       seeming sweet,

[170]

but a brother's death
            drove a young man's kickshaws
into limbo –
            I have lost you, my brother
and your death has ended
            the spring season
of my happiness,
            our house is buried with you
& buried the laughter that you taught me.
There are no thoughts of love nor of poems
in my head
            since you died.
Hence, Manlius
            the reproach in your Roman letter
leaves me unmoved:
            "Why loiter in Verona,
Catullus, where
            for men of our circle
cold limbs in an empty bed
            are the rule –
not the exception?"
            Forgive me, my friend
but the dalliance of love
            that you look for
has been soured by mourning.
            As for a poem . . .
our tastes call for my Greek books,
            and those are at home
where we both live
            and where our years pile up,
in Rome . . .
            I have few copies of anything by me.

One case only has followed me North.
There is nothing curmudgeonly here –
on whom do you think
   I would sooner lavish
love-gifts of Venus
   & gifts of the Holy Muses
than you?
   You have turned to a friend
& the friend's hands are empty. . . .
How can I give what I have not got?

   ★ ★ ★ ★ ★

And yet
   lest 'Oblivion's veil'
descend
   too early on your kindness
it is right
   that the Nine Sisters
should know of my debt,
   Manlius,
they will repeat
   the words in this scroll
to unborn generations,
   your name will grow brighter
as the paper yellows,
   while the subtle spider
fails to hang
   his delicate filaments
over a neglected name.

My harrowing
   at the hands of Venus

[172]

(whom no man should ever trust)
        is well-known
in Pieria –
        how I burned like Aetnaean lava,
how I boiled like the hot springs at Thermopylae,
tears ceaselessly in my stricken eyes,
my cheeks drenched with lamentable showers,
and then, Manlius,
        as a hill stream
unexpectedly springing
        from a wind-clear crest
exchanging
        the mossed boulders
of its source
        for the steep-sloped gully
where it plunges
        precipitously
to the valley floor
        you appeared
& brought
        (with your friend's kindness)
the refreshment to me
        that the stream brings to the fissured vineyards
heavy under the hot sun
        & to the sweat-worn *contadini*
who work in them.
        You came
as the Dioscuri
        in the black-breathed storm
conjuring the right wind from the right quarter,
as Castor at the sailors' prayer,
as Pollux at the sailors' prayer.

[173]

You opened a path
        where the field had been shut before.
You gave a roof to our love,
        whose Mistress connived
at our *rencontres*
        & the love-ease that we sought there.
With supple steps
        Catullus's bright-shining Goddess
found her way thither,
        her woman's sandals
echoing
        on the worn threshold-stone.

Thus . . .
        with as flagrant desire
Laodamia
        came to Protesilaus
crossing the marriage threshold
of a house doomed to stand empty,
the blood-tribute neglected . . .
the Lords of Hill-Heaven unappeased.
Shield me,
        Rhamnusian Queen
from like joy-hastes
        by-passing Heaven
Laodamia
        learnt too well
in her swift widowing
        the thirst
of holy altars
        for their blood-due:
before the first & second winters

[174]

with their lovers' nights
        had satisfied
her bride's love-greed
& made the shattered wedding-yoke
endurable,
        her arms unclasped
her husband's neck
        who sailed for Trojan walls
and fell
        as Fate foresaw
the first to land.

For Helen's rape
        had driven Greece to arms,
Troy was the cause,
        & Troy spread death –
a common grave for the young of Asia & Achaia.
The crowds of fighting-men
        & the feats-of-arms
found their end there,
        and you, who shone in my life,
who are stretched now by the same headland . . .
I have lost you, my brother,
        your death has ended
the spring season
        of my happiness,
our house is buried with you,
& buried the laughter that you taught me.
You lie under alien ground
        among anonymous tombs
far from our reach
        far from our house-clan grave mounds:

[175]

the malign fields of the Troad cover your ashes.
There gathered
                    the Argive Princes
hurriedly leaving
                    home, fields & hearth
lest in an easeful bed
                    Paris
unchallenged, enjoy
                    the limbs of the Spartan woman
whom he had stolen.

                    This was the history
of your loss
                    Laodamia
who were the loveliest of the brides of Thessaly,
whose husband was sweeter to you
                    than your own life
whom you loved as completely
                    as the water the whirlpool,
the love-pit in your soul
                    – deep as Lake Zerithon,
where Hercules hacked out the caverns under Cyllene
& drained the Stymphalian swamp of its silt waters,
when the first & the least born,
                    Eurystheus,
set him to slaughter
                    the man-eating cranes
which Jove's son picked-off
                    with his death-bolts,
& was half-way to Heaven. . . .
                    A new god

to come & go on Olympus –
    where Hebe,
the cup-bearer,
      already half-fears
for her virgin days.
    Far deeper
than such gulfs of love
      was yours, that taught
an untamed girl
    to wear
with freedom the wedlock yoke. . . .
    Love
was not more of a miracle
      for the old man with money
& an only daughter
      who, at the last minute,
produces a grandson . . .
    the family wealth
is secured,
      the child's name
inserted & witnessed in the will,
while the vulturine relatives
observed to have been perched
expectantly
      on grandpapa's grey poll
flap off
    discomfited.
No dove
    uxoriously
enjoyed its snow-white mate
with more promiscuous beak
    than you

collecting bites for kisses,
> though doves
(they say)
> are more omnivorous
than women
> when their appetites are stung.
Yet these
> beside your violence
fail,
> confronted by a fair-haired man,
Protesilaus. . . .

And the light of Catullus's own life
when she looked for his embrace
> gave little
in the matter of passion
> to you, Laodamia.
Cupid was clothed in saffron
> & shone & played
in her love-movements . . .
> who looks (it is true)
elsewhere
> for other love.
But the quests are few & secret.
I hold my tongue, remembering
that cuckolds are a tedious lot –
Juno herself
> faced with all-loving Jove's
interminable *amours*
> digests her rage. . . .
Yet men & gods make poor comparisons.

Why, like a husband, should I ape the father?
No father yielded me this daughter,
Who comes to my house
         by night
shedding Assyrian perfumes
         her husband unaware
of the love-charms that she brings me. . . .
I ask for no more,
         enough that her sweet thefts
mark white days in the calendar of my love.

        ★   ★   ★   ★   ★

Thus, Manlius,
         for the 'offices of friendship'
you have shown me,
         this gift of a poem –
not perhaps what you asked for
         but what I can do . . .
it will help
         to ward off the rust of successive years
from your name,
         & the gods will also reward you
& Themis
         who ever in the old days
kept an eye on the worthy.
         May happiness clothe you
& the woman who comforts you –
even the house of our love-games
         & its Mistress,
& he who first brought us together
the fount of so much that was good in our lives.

But beyond these
          always she
who is dearer to me than all else,
my light & my eyes
          who, living,
invests life for Catullus
          with its sweet reason.

69

Do not wonder when the wench declines
your thigh her thigh to place beneath.
You cannot buy them with the costliest clothes
or with extravagance of clearest stones.
There's an ugly rumour abroad,
     b.o. under the armpits –
and nobody likes that!
    So do not wonder if
a nice girl declines the goat-pit.
Either reach for the deodorant,
or cease to wonder that she so declines.

70

Lesbia says she'ld rather marry me
than anyone,
      though Jupiter himself came asking
or so she says,
      but what a woman tells her lover in desire
should be written out on air & running water.

71

If ever anyone
was deservedly plagued by a goat under his armpits
or crippled with gout,
                          your rival
who performs gratuitously on the body of your love
would appear remarkably handicapped by both complaints.
Whenever they do it, you're avenged on the pair of them:
she passes out at once under the malodour,
he's bent double in an ecstasy of gout.

72

There was a time, Lesbia, when
you confessed only to Catullus in love:
you would set me above Jupiter himself.
I loved you then
          not as men love their women
but as a father his children – his family.
To-day I know you too well
          and desire burns deeper in me
and you are more coarse
          more frivolous in my thought.
"How," you may ask, "can this be?"
Such actions as yours excite
          increased violence of love,
Lesbia, but with friendless intention.

73

Cancel, Catullus, the expectancies of friendship
cancel the kindnesses deemed to accrue there:
kindness is barren, friendship breeds nothing,
only the weight of past deeds growing oppressive
as Catullus has discovered, bitter & troubled,
in one he had once accounted a unique friend.

74

Gellius,
            hearing his uncle anathematise the mere mention
as well as the performance of love and love's ways
determined to take full advantage of the situation
by promptly assaulting his aunt. Uncle
was discreetly unable even to refer to the event.
Gellius could do as he wished.
            If he buggered the old man himself,
Uncle would not utter a word.

75

Reason blinded by sin, Lesbia,
a mind drowned in its own devotion:
come clothed in your excellences –
I cannot think tenderly of you,
sink to what acts you dare –
I can never cut this love.

76

If evocations of past kindness shed
ease in the mind of one of rectitude,
of bond inviolate, who never in abuse of God
led men intentionally to harm,
such, as life lasts, must in Catullus shed
effect of joy from disregarded love.
For what by man can well in act or word
be done to others has by me been done
sunk in the credit of an unregarding heart.
Why protract this pain? why not resist
yourself in mind; from this point inclining
yourself back, breaking this fallen love
counter to what the gods desire of men?
Hard suddenly to lose love of long use,
hard precondition of your sanity
regained. Possible or not, this last
conquest is for you to make, Catullus.
May the pitying gods who bring
help to the needy at the point of death
look towards me and, if my life were clean,
tear this malign pest out from my body
where, a paralysis, it creeps from limb to limb
driving all former laughter from the heart.
I do not now expect – or want – my love returned,
nor cry to the moon for Lesbia to be chaste:
only that the gods cure me of this disease
and, as I once was whole, make me now whole again.

77

Whom I have trusted to no end (Rufus)
other than expense of evil knowledge
has come to the ambush,
     inflamed viscera,
raped all that was precious.
Here was poison in rape of life
     here was disease of love.
Witness the chaste mouth of a chaste woman
soiled by loathsome saliva –
     not with impunity:
your acts shall to succeeding ages
be by the bent Sibyl broadcast, in accents of infamy.

78

Gallus's brothers possess
> one, the most attractive of wives
the other, an equally attractive son.
Gallus is a 'dear'
> arranging soft love for the lovers
putting the beautiful boy & the beautiful wife into bed
> together.
Gallus is myopic:
> himself a husband –
giving a young lad lessons in cuckoldry!

79

They nickname Lesbia's brother 'pulcher',
    naturally
since she prefers him to Catullus & the Catulli;
but let him dispose as he will of Catullus
    (& the Catulli)
when he finds three men of distinction
    willing to greet him in public.

80

How is it, Gellius,
        when you leave home in the morning
& again at 2 in the afternoon
        with the rest of the day before you
after your soft siesta
        that your lips
previously pink
        are unaccountably whiter than winter snow?
One is not sure,
        unless rumour speak true:
that you swallow the taut tumescence of a man's stomach.
One thing is certain
        that Virro's strained thighs
& the white marks on your lips
cry out in unison to onlookers.

81

Surely, Iuventius, one of this throng in Rome
must be more to your taste than your present guest
whose skin is the colour of old ivory
who comes from Pesaro
      a provincial backwater,
whom you've placed now in your heart,
whom you dare hold up to Catullus,
unaware of your solecism?

82

My eyes in your pledge, Quintius,
and something more precious than eyes to me;
do not touch what is more precious than my eyes,
more treasured than something more precious than precious eyes.

83

Lesbia is extraordinarily vindictive
about me in front of her husband
who is thereby moved to fatuous laughter –
a man mulishly insensitive, failing to grasp
that a mindless silence (about me) spells safety
while to spit out my name in curses, baring
her white teeth, means she remembers me, and
what is more pungent still, is scratching the wound
ripening herself while she talks.

84

'*H*advantageous' breathes Arrius heavily
          when he means 'advantageous',
intending 'artificial' he labours '*h*artificial',
convinced he is speaking impeccably while
he blows his 'h's about most '*h*artificially'.
One understands that his mother – his uncle –
his family, in fact, on the distaff side
spoke so.
         Fortunately he was posted to Syria
and our ears grew accustomed to normal speech again,
unapprehensive for a while of such words
until suddenly the grotesque news reaches us
that the Ionian Sea has become
             since the advent of Arrius
no longer Ionian
      but (inevitably) *H*ionian.

85

I hate and I love. And if you ask me how,
I do not know: I only feel it, and I'm torn in two.

86

We have heard of Quintia's beauty. To me she is tall,
  slender
and of a white 'beauty'. Such things I freely admit;
but such things do not constitute beauty.
      In her there is nothing of Venus,
not a pinch of love spice in her long body.
While Lesbia, Lesbia is loveliness indeed.
      Herself of particular beauty
has she not plundered womanhead of all its graces,
      flaunting them as her adornment?

87

No woman loved, in truth, Lesbia
as you by me;
no love-faith found so true
as mine in you.

88

What, Gellius, of the man
who itches with sister & mother
        naked in night-vigils,
who 'lies-in' for his uncle,
what stain does he lay on himself?
Such, that not Tethys to far limits
nor Ocean, father of Nereids, can cleanse:
no fouler brand (Gellius)
        even supposing
demisso se ipse voret capite.

89

Gellius is thin.
        So?
             He possesses
an unusually agreeable mother
a similarly compliant uncle
a sister swelling with Venus
and a whole crowd of female 'connections
– Is he likely to put on much weight?

A taste for his sort of forbidden fruit
is no way to wax plump.

90

Let there stem (Gellius)
from the execrable conjunction of a son with his mother
a Magus skilled in Persian priestcraft, for such
if the unnatural cults of the Near East are correct
must the seed be (Gellius) of mother & son:
such only can summon the gods in song
when the grease of entrail-fat flares on the altar.

91

In this hopeless & wasting love of mine
I trusted you for one reason, Gellius:
not because I knew you well
            nor respected your constancy
nor thought you able (or willing) to rinse out your mind
but merely because the woman for whom
this compulsive desire is eating me
happens to be neither your mother
            nor sister
nor any other close female relative.
In spite of our intimacy I did not believe
you would find here incentive for action.
– You did,
            in the overwhelming attraction
pure sin holds for you, Gellius,
            or anything smacking of sin.

92

Lesbia loads me night & day with her curses,
'Catullus' always on her lips,
      yet I know that she loves me.
How? I equally spend myself day & night
in assiduous execration
      – knowing too well my hopeless love.

93

Utter indifference to your welfare, Caesar,
is matched only by ignorance of who you are.

94

Stuffing, O'Toole naturally stuffs with his tool:
the stew-pot stews in its own mess.

95

Nine harvests & nine winters since its inception
Cinna's *Zmyrna* is complete.
Hortalus turns out 5,000 versicles yearly.
Penetrating to the runnelled waves of Satrachus
the remote regions of its setting,
      Cinna's *Zmyrna*
shall be read by white-haired generations.
The *Annals* of Volusius will wilt by the banks of the Padua,
occasionally a limp wrapping for mackerel.
Cinna's lapidary relics are to Catullus' taste:
let the public plump for the fustian of Antimachus.

96

If, Calvus, effects of grief
     affect
those enigmatic sepulchres
     of former love
& spent friendships,
     lamented & evoked in our desire,
reflect, her early death
     will never grieve Quintilia
half so much
     as your long love must make her gay.

97

As God is my witness where is the difference between
the smell of Aemilius' mouth & that of his arse?
The cleanness of one equals the filth of the other. Actually
his arse is probably the cleaner & nicer of the two:
there he's without teeth, while the teeth in his mouth
are half a yard long, stuck in the gums like an old wagon
behind them the cleft cunt of a she-mule pissing in summer.
And this Being copulates.
                            A fit dolt for the treadmill.
Considers himself an object of elegance.
Whatever woman handles this man is equally
capable of licking the arse-hole of a leprous hangman.

98

The same can be said of you, Victius
as of any open-mouthed bore
                              suffering from halitosis.
With that tongue of yours one can actually credit
your licking, at will, besmeared boots & buttocks.
If you wish to prostrate the company –
                                          gape:
you will effectively accomplish your purpose

99

Purloining while you played in honeyed youth
a kiss, sweeter than one suspects ambrosia tastes,
I paid, Iuventius, in full:
                                          an hour or more
you racked me with my own self-exculpations
your loathing left untouched by tears.
No sooner had I kissed you
                                          than with every finger
in every corner of your mouth
                                          you washed & rubbed
all contact of my lips
                                          like the slaver of some syphilitic whore
away. More:
                      you gave me, fallen, to an enemy
                                                      – Amor
who has not since ceased to rack me in his own usage,
so that a purloined kiss
                                          once ambrosial,
is changed to one more acid than acid hellbane tastes.
Met with such strong despite of love
                                                      my fallen love
shall from this day no kisses more purloin.

100

Undone or done up with love
Caelius for Aufilenus
        Quintius for Aufilena
that for the brother
        this for the sister
each the flower of young Verona,
something beyond 'brotherly love' . . .
which should I favour, Caelius, but you
who showed me such friendship when
the irrational flame seared me
in Rome? Be happy, Caelius. Thrive.
        Be potent in loving.

101

Journeying over many seas & through many countries
I come dear brother to this pitiful leave-taking
the last gestures by your graveside
the futility of words over your quiet ashes.
Life cleft us from each other
pointlessly depriving brother of brother.
Accept then, in our parents' custom
these offerings, this leave-taking
echoing for ever, brother, through a brother's tears.

                                        – 'Hail & Farewell'.

102

If, Cornelius, we entrust our secrets
only to those whom we know we can trust,
here is Catullus,
      devoted to secrets & secrecy
a finger ever to his lips,
      as mute as Harpocrates!

103

Either give me my hundred pounds back, Silo
and persist in your boorish, surly behaviour, or
if as a guide to tarts the money tempts you,
simply give up your boorish, surly behaviour.

104

Do you really believe I could blacken my life,
the woman dearer to me than my two eyes?
If I could
      I should not be sunk in this way in my love for her –

who performs a zoo of two-backed beasts,
daily with Tappo.

105

O'Toole
    attempting an entry of the *mons Parnassus*
is pitchforked by the Muses out of their (very) private
    regions.

106

When an auctioneer's seen with a good-looking boy
      (by himself)
it is fair to presume that there has been purchase & sale
     – in a closed market.

107

If ever anyone anywhere, Lesbia, is looking
            for what he knows will not happen
and then unexpectedly it happens –
                        the soul is astonished,
as we are now in each other,
                        an event dearer than gold,
for you have restored yourself, Lesbia, desired
restored yourself, longed for, unlooked for,
                            brought yourself back
to me. White day in the calendar!
                        Who happier than I?
What more can life offer
   than the longed for unlooked for event when it happens?

108

If, by general consent, it should be decided
Cominius, to cut short your reverend age
fouled by obscene habits,
      I envisage your tongue
inimical to the good
      extracted & cast to the crows,
your gouged eyeballs
      gulped down the black gullet of a raven,
entrails offal for dogs,
      your limbs to the wolves.

109

Joy of my life! you tell me this –
that nothing can possibly break this love of ours for each
   other.

God let her mean what she says,
                          from a candid heart,
that our two lives may be linked in their length
day to day,
          each to each,
in a bond of sacred fidelity.

110

Men always praise an honest whore, keen
for the price of what she proposes to do,
but to promise & break promise
                frequently taking & never giving
proves the woman, Aufilena, inimical to men.
Keep either your words or your modesty intact:
perform what you offer,
                or don't make the offer at all.
To take fraudulent payment proves you
worse than the tart who avariciously
prostitutes herself with every part of her body.

III

In constancy content with one man, there
Aufilena, is the epitome of bridehood; yet
sooner your thigh put to promiscuous use
than that the one man be your uncle
and you begetting from him your own first cousins.

112

Naso! an elevated personage
with a stoop, however, bespeaking
a somewhat different sort of 'elevation'.
Indeed, an elevated person.

113

In The Year of Pompey's First Consulate, Cinna,
two men 'frequented' the First Lady,
In The Year of Pompey's Second Consulate
the same two are still at it,
but now with a cohort of others:
adultery spreads like a weed.

114

O'Toole is generally accounted
a wealthy man,
       fish fowl game
meadow & plough land,
       the broad acres near Firmum
packed with abundance.
       To what purpose?
Its owner spends more than he makes.
I salute such riches
       more apparent than real,
I praise the estate
       whose owner is lacking in substance.

115

O'Toole is the proud master of
20 acres of pasture
        & 27 acres of arable land
the rest is unfortunately swamp.
Where is our latter-day Croesus
the man loaded with such an estate,
grass plough wood moor & marsh land
stretching away to the Hyperborean North
and down to the shores of the Adriatic?
Everything here's on a grand scale
including the owner,
        and he's not a man either,
but a *tool* larger than life,
        upreared & rampant at the gates!

116

Conscientiously bringing my mind to bear on this
   problem
Gellius,
        I have thought more than once
that the example of Callimachus
        his songs sent you from me
might ease our relations
        dissuade you from bombarding me
with offensive squibs,
        all of which, I can see now,
was wasted hope & effort.
        Your darts we shall continue to parry
– with a pass of the cloak,
        while in our epigrams you stand
transfixed in ignominy.

GLOSSARY OF PROPER NAMES

Names of geographical features and/or familiar place-names which have remained constant, or nearly so, have not been included. Where necessary, substantival forms have been substituted for adjectival ones. The letter 'L', in brackets, stands for 'Lemprière', to whose eminently traditional work the reader is referred for further information.

ACHAIA. Another name for Hellas; a synonym for Greece. (Poem 68)

ACHILLES. (L.) Son of Peleus and Thetis. One of the mightiest of the Greek heroes in the Trojan War. (Poem 64)

ADONIS. (L.) A mortal youth of great beauty who was loved by Venus. (Poem 29)

AEGEUS. (L.) The father of Theseus and King of Athens. Believing his son to have been killed by the Minotaur, he threw himself into the sea, which was subsequently named the Aegean. (Poem 64)

AEMILIUS. Unidentified. (Poem 97)

AESOP. (L.) The sixth-century philosopher and fabulist who, according to tradition, lived at the court of King Croesus. (Poem 28)

AGANIPPE. One of the two springs on Mount Helicon, which were sacred to the Muses. Hippocrene was the other. (Poem 61)

ALECTO. One of the three Furies. (Poem 64)

ALFENUS. Traditionally, P. Alfenus Varus (q.v.). (Poems 10, 30)

AMASTRIS. A port near Cytorus (q.v.), and similarly situated. (Poem 4)

AMATHUSIA. Another name for Cyprus, where Venus was particularly worshipped. (Poem 36)

AMEANA. Either Mamurra's mistress, or a prostitute with whom he had dealings. Poem 41 implies she was a Cisalpine. (Poem 41)

AMMON. (L.) The present-day oasis of Siwa in Libya. The Egyptian god Ammon was worshipped there as 'Jupiter Ammon'. (Poem 7)

AMOR. Cupid (q.v.). (Poems 45, 99)

AMPHITRITE. One of the Nereids, hence the sea. (Poem 64)

ANCON. Latin, Ancona. A town on the Adriatic coast, originally a Greek colony associated with Venus. (Poem 36)

[229]

ANDROGEOS. (L.) Son of Minos and Pasiphaë, murdered, by Aegeus, on account of his athletic prowess at the Panathenaic games. (Poem 64)

ANTIMACHUS. (L.) A sixth-century poet, author of an epic poem on the Theban War. In his own day his work was rated second only to that of Homer. (Poem 95)

ANTIUS. Unidentified; apparently involved in a law-suit in which P. Sestius was the prosecutor. (Poem 44)

AONIA. A name for Boeotia. Mount Helicon is situated there. (Poem 61)

APÁME. Berenice's mother, the wife of Magas, King of Cyrene. On her husband's death, she cancelled her daughter's engagement to Ptolemy III (246-221 B.C.), and arranged for her to marry his cousin, Demetrius, who, however, devoted his attentions to Apáme rather than Berenice, for which, under Berenice's personal direction, he was assassinated in Apáme's bedroom. Berenice subsequently married Ptolemy III. (Poem 66)

APELIOTA. The East Wind. (Poem 26)

APOLLO. (L.) Often referred to as 'Phoebus' Apollo, and thus identified with the sun, but his sphere of activity is wide. He is patron of the arts, sciences and all civilised activity. He is the son of Jupiter and Latona, and the twin of Diana. (Poem 64)

AQUINUS. A poet of the old-fashioned traditionalist school. He may be the Aquinus mentioned by Cicero in his *Tusculan Disputations* v. 63. (Poem 14)

ARGIVES. (L.) The crew of the Argo; also the inhabitants of the city of Argos, the capital of Argolis, in which sense the word is a synonym for 'Greeks'. (Poem 64)

ARIADNE. (L.) The daughter of Minos and Pasiphaë. She helped Theseus to kill the Minotaur, who was her half-brother. She and Theseus subsequently eloped; but he abandoned her on the island of Naxos. There she was consoled by Bacchus, who married her, bringing as a wedding present the Corona of seven stars, which bears her name. (Poems 64, 66)

ARRIUS. Traditionally, the self-made Q. Arrius, praetor and supporter of M. Crassus, whom he possibly accompanied to Parthia, a journey which would have entailed an Ionian crossing, such as is referred to in the poem. (Poem 84)

ARSÍNOE. (L.) Berenice's mother-in-law, the wife of Ptolemy II (283–246 B.C.). She was deified and worshipped as a manifestation of Aphrodite. (Poem 66)

ARTEMIS. Latin, Diana (L.), Apollo's twin, virgin goddess of the moon and of hunting. (Poem 64)

ASINIUS. Asinius Marrucinus, brother of C. Asinius Pollio (*q.v.*). (Poem 12)

ATHENE. Latin, Minerva (L.). Goddess of war and wisdom, protectress of Athens. She was said to have sprung fully armed from Jove's head. (Poem 64)

ATTIS. (L.) Archetypal devotee of the Mother Goddess. (Poem 63)

AUFILENUS/AUFILENA. Unidentified, presumably a Veronese brother and sister. (Poems 100, 110, 111)

AURELIUS. Unidentified, possibly a Cisalpine like Furius with whom he is coupled. (Poems 11, 15, 16, 21)

AURORA. (L.) The Dawn. (Poem 64)

AURUNCULEIA, Vinia (*q.v.*). (Poem 61)

BACCHUS. (L.) The God of wine who was the object of an ecstatic cult, similar in many respects to that of Cybele. (Poems 27, 64)

BALBUS. An unidentified Veronese. (Poem 67)

BATTIADES. A descendant of King Battus, a Spartan who built the Libyan city of Cyrene in 630 B.C., and became its first king. The term was used as a patronymic for Callimachus (*q.v.*). (Poem 7)

BERECYNTHIA. A mountain in Phrygia, associated with the worship of Cybele. (Poem 63)

BERENICE. (L.) Wife of Ptolemy III. Soon after her marriage her husband left for a campaign in Syria. Berenice placed a lock of her hair in her mother-in-law's shrine at Zephyrium, against his safe return. Unfortunately the lock was lost. The Royal Astronomer, Conon, was consulted, and discovered it as a new constellation, the Coma Berenices. Callimachus wrote a poem to celebrate the event. (Poems 65, 66)

BIBACULUS. M. Furius Bibaculus, a Cremonese, one of the 'new poets'.

BITHYNIA. A Roman province on the south-western shores of the Black Sea. (Poems 10, 25, 31)

BOÖTES. The constellation of Arcturus. (Poem 66)

CAECILIUS. Unidentified, presumably a Cisalpine. The name appears in poems 35 and 67, and may or may not refer to the same person.

CAELIUS. M. Caelius Rufus (*q.v.*). (Poems 58, 100)

CAESAR. (L.) C. Julius Caesar, the dictator; the object of some of Catullus's most virulent epigrams in which the poet ridicules his reputed pederasty and his patronage of Mamurra. (Poems 11, 54, 57, 93)

CAESIUS. An unidentified poet but, like Aquinus, with whom he is linked, evidently a follower of the traditionalist school. (Poem 14)

CALLIMACHUS. (L.) The Greek poet, a native of Cyrene (died 250 B.C.). He lived at Alexandria where he worked in the Library. He was especially admired by the poets of Catullus's circle and wrote the elegant piece of court poetry of which poem 66 is a direct translation. (Poems 65, 116)

CALVUS. C. Licinius Calvus, poet and orator; a close friend of Catullus and a colleague of Cicero. As a writer he is linked by Ovid with Catullus and Tibullus. He was probably a small man, *vide* the last line of poem 53. (Poems 14, 50, 53, 96)

CAMERIUS. Unidentified. (Poem 55)

CASTOR. (L.) One of the Dioscuri (*q.v.*). (Poems 4, 68)

CATO. Almost certainly P. Valerius Cato, a Veronese freedman, born *c.*100 B.C., poet and man of letters. His influence on his younger contemporaries appears to have been great. He may well have been the original source of the new movement in poetry. (Poem 56)

CATULLUS. C. Valerius Catullus (*c.* 84 – *c.* 54 B.C.), a Veronese who lived in Rome and was one of the principal figures of the new school of poetry referred to disparagingly by Cicero as 'the moderns'. They sought to apply Alexandrian criticism and technique to Latin poetry. Catullus is known to have visited Asia Minor for a year, and to have lost a brother in the same part of the world. He was a member of Clodia's circle, and was accepted by her as one of her lovers. (Poems 2, 6, 7, 8, 9, 12, 14, 15, 21, 28, 30, 31, 35, 40, 42, 44, 46, 49, 51, 52, 55, 56, 58, 63, 67, 68, 72, 73, 76, 79, 81, 92, 95, 102)

CHALYBES. (L.) The inhabitants of a region in Asia Minor, near Pontus which was celebrated for its iron mines. (Poem 66)

CHIRON. (L.) The Centaur, Peleus's grandfather and the future tutor of Achilles. He lived on the slopes of Mount Pelion. (Poem 64)

CICERO. (L.) M. Tullius Cicero, the orator, statesman and author. His year as consul coincided with the Cataline conspiracy. He incurred the enmity of Caesar's faction and was driven into exile by P. Clodius Pulcher. His speech *Pro Caelio*, defending M. Caelius Rufus, provides us with the only full-length portrait of Clodia. Although he was an intimate of many of Catullus's friends, poem 49 is the only direct link between the two to have been preserved.

CIEROS. A town in Thessaly. (Poem 64)

CINNA. C. Helvius Cinna, a Cisalpine and friend of Catullus; one of the 'new poets'. He probably accompanied Catullus, under the patronage of C. Memmius, to Bithynia. He was murdered in the confusion after Caesar's death in mistake for Cinna the conspirator, as in Shakespeare's play. (Poems 10, 95, 113)

CLIVUS VICTORIAE. The exclusive residential street on the Palatine, where Clodia and her brother lived. (Poem 37)

CLODIA. (L.) Clodia Metelli, the wife of Q. Metellus Celer, her cousin. She was reputed to have innumerable lovers and, on her husband's death, was suspected of having poisoned him. Much of Catullus's most vitriolic as well as some of his tenderest poetry was inspired by her.

CNIDOS. A city in Caria in which there were three temples dedicated to Venus. (Poem 36)

COLCHIS. (L.) A region at the far end of the Black Sea. The Argonauts sailed to Colchis, to obtain the Golden Fleece. (Poem 64)

COLOGNA VENETA. A small town near Verona. There used to be a bridge there called *Il Ponte di Catullo*. (Poem 17)

COLOSSUS. (L.) An immense bronze statue a hundred and five feet high, straddling the entrance to the harbour of Rhodes. It was known as one of the wonders of the world. (Poem 4)

COMINIUS. Unidentified. (Poem 108)

CORNELIUS. Cornelius Nepos (*q.v.*). (Poems 1, 67, 102)

CORNIFICIUS. Q. Cornificius, the quaestor (48 B.C.), who espoused the Senatorial cause and was killed in battle in 41. He was one of the 'new poets', a friend of Catullus and Cicero. (Poem 38)

CRANNON. One of the principal towns of Thessaly. (Poem 64)

CROESUS. (L.) The fabulously rich king of Lydia. (Poem 115)

CUPID. (L.) The son of Venus, traditionally armed with bow and arrows, who inspires the victims of his archery with erotic passion. In the plural, 'the spirits of love'. (Poems 3, 13, 36, 64, 68)

CYBEBE. Another name for Cybele (*q.v.*). In poem 63, Catullus uses both forms, the first 'e' of 'Cybebe' being long, and that of 'Cybele' short.

CYBELE. (L.) The Mother Goddess. Her cult, which was ecstatic, was of Phrygian origin. It reached Greece in the sixth century B.C., and was introduced into Rome in the Second Punic War. Her temple stood on the Palatine, behind Clodia's house. (Poem 35)

CYCLADES. A group of islands in the Aegean. (Poem 4)

CYCNEA. An old fortress dominating Brescia. (Poem 67)

CYLLENE. A mountain in Arcadia on whose slopes there was a town of the same name. (Poem 68)

CYNTHIA. Another name for Diana (*q.v.*). (Poem 66)

CYTHEREA. (L.) The adjectival form of 'Cythera', the modern Cerigo, an island off the coast of Laconia. According to some authorities, it was the scene of Venus's emergence from the sea. Hence, she was often called 'Cytherea'. (Poem 66)

CYTORUS. A port in Paphlagonia on the borders of Bithynia. It lay at the foot of a mountain of the same name, famous for its boxwood. (Poem 4)

DARDANIA. Another name for the Troad (*q.v.*). (Poem 65)

DELOS. An island in the Cyclades, holy to Diana, who was said to have been born there. (Poem 34)

DELPHOS. (L.) A city in Phocis, said to be situated at the centre of the earth. Its Bacchantes, or female worshippers of Bacchus, were called 'Thyiades'. (Poem 64)

DIANA. (L.) Virgin goddess of the moon and of hunting. (Poem 34)

DINDYMIA. A mountain in Phrygia, associated with Cybele. Hence, another name for the goddess. (Poem 63)

DIOSCURI. Castor and Pollux, twin sons of Jupiter, who protect sailors in times of storm. They constitute the zodiacal sign of Gemini. (Poems 4, 57, 68)

EGNATIUS. Unidentified. (Poems 37, 39)

EMATHIA. Another name for Thessaly, birthplace of Achilles. (Poem 64)

ENDYMION. A mortal youth loved by Diana. In order to keep him to herself she confined him to a cave on Mount Latmos and condemned him to a state of perpetual sleep. (Poem 66)

EPIDAMNUS. The Roman Dyrrachium, modern Durres, a busy crossing-place on the Adriatic. A thriving port would indicate a thriving cult of Venus, hence the reference in poem 36.

ERINYES. (L.) The three Furies. They hound those who disregard natural law, whether intentionally or otherwise. (Poem 64)

ERIUS. An unidentified intimate of Caesar. (Poem 54)

ERYX. A mountain on the west coast of Sicily, where there was a temple dedicated to Venus. (Poem 64)

EUROPA. (L.) The mother, by Jove, of Minos King of Crete. The god appeared to her in the shape of a bull, carried her to Crete and secured her there under the guardianship of the bronze giant, Talus. (Poem 55)

EUROTAS. A river in Laconia, not far from Sparta. (Poem 64)

EURYSTHEUS. (L.) The cousin of Hercules, who was subject to him. It was Eurystheus who ordered Hercules to perform his twelve labours. (Poem 68)

EUXINE LAKE. The Black Sea. (Poem 64)

FABULLUS. Unidentified. He apparently served in Spain, and possibly in Macedonia, in the same sort of capacity as Catullus himself in Bithynia. He is coupled with Veranius. (Poems 12, 13, 28, 47)

FALERNIAN. A type of wine. (Poem 27)

FIRMUM. A town in Picenum, near which Mamurra had an estate. (Poem 114)

FLAVIUS. Unidentified. (Poem 6)

FORMIANUS. Mamurra (*q.v.*). (Poems 41, 43)

FURIUS. Probably M. Furius Bibaculus (*q.v.*). (Poems 11, 16, 23, 24, 26)

GALLAE. (L.) The priests of Cybele, so called from the river Gallus in Phrygia, whose waters maddened those who drank from it.

[235]

The Gallae, as a final service to the goddess, castrated themselves during her rite, hence the dramatic change of sex in the poem. (Poem 63)

GALLUS. Unidentified. (Poem 78)

GELLIUS. L. Gellius Poplicola (*q.v.*). (Poems 74, 80, 88, 89, 90, 91, 116)

GOLGOS. Golgi, a town in Cyprus, associated with Venus. (Poems 36, 64)

GUA. The river at Cologna Veneta, once spanned by the *Ponte di Catullo*. (Poem 17)

HAMADRYADS. Tree nymphs, whose life is the physical life of the tree. (Poem 61)

HARPOCRATES. (L.) Horus, the Egyptian child-god of silence. (Poem 102)

HEBE. (L.) Goddess of eternal youth, who was conceived by Juno as the result of a diet of lettuces. She became Hercules's wife after his apotheosis. (Poem 68)

HECAT. (L.) Also called Trivia, since her presence is particularly felt where three roads met. She represents the moon on the wane and, as such, is one of the aspects of Diana. She conducts the souls of dead women to Hades. (Poem 34)

HELEN. (L.) The most beautiful woman in the world, the wife of Menelaus King of Sparta. Her abduction by Paris was the immediate cause of the Trojan War. (Poem 68)

HELICON. A mountain in Boeotia, the home of the Muses and of Hymen. (Poem 61)

HERCULES. (L.) Jove's son by Alcmena. He was the greatest of mortal heroes, celebrated for his twelve labours and subsequent apotheosis. He was also one of the Argonauts. (Poems 55, 68)

HORTALUS (L.) Q. Hortensius Hortalus, praetor and consul, died 50 B.C., a distinguished lawyer and friend of Cicero. Although one of the 'new poets' and the recipient of poems 65 and 66, his verse does not appear to have met with Catullus's approval: *vide* poem 95.

HYMEN. (L.) Also Hymenaeus. The god of marriage, who lives on Mount Helicon in the company of the Muses. (Poems 61, 62, 64)

HYPERBOREI. (L.) A race who lived beyond the region where the North Wind starts to blow, said to be in Thrace. (Poem 115)

HYRCANIA. A wild and desolate country of Asia. (Poem 11)

IDA. (L.) A mountain in the Troad, which was originally part of Phrygia (poem 63), and also (poem 64), a mountain in Crete.

IDALIA. A district in Cyprus where there was a grove sacred to Venus. (Poems 36, 64)

IPSÍTHILLA. Unidentified. From the poem (32), almost certainly not a prostitute in our sense, but more likely a hetæra, or a freed-woman, whom Catullus knew.

ITYLUS. The Homeric name for Itys (L.), son of Tereus and Procne (q.v.). He was killed by his mother, who gave him to his father to eat after she had learnt that Tereus had violated her sister. (Poem 65)

IUVENTIUS. Unidentified. (Poems 24, 48, 81, 99)

JOVE. Jupiter (q.v.). (Poems 7, 64, 67, 68)

JUNO. (L.) Queen of Heaven, Jove's wife and sister. (Poems 64, 68)

JUNO LUCINA. Patron of childbirth, an aspect of Diana* (L.). (Poem 34)

JUPITER. (L.) The father of the gods, and lord of the upper regions, as his two brothers, Neptune and Pluto, are of the sea and the underworld respectively. Neptune was believed to have built the walls of Troy. (Poems 70, 72)

LADAS. One of Alexander the Great's couriers, who ran so swiftly that he left no footprints. (Poem 55)

LAMPSACUS. (L.) A town near the Dardanelles, noted for its oysters and its devotion to Priapus. (Poem 18)

LANUVIUM. A town in Latium. (Poem 39)

LAODAMIA. (L.) The wife of Protesilaus. She was so distressed by the loss of her husband, which occurred almost immediately after their marriage, that she had a life-size statue made of him, which she kept concealed in her bed, and with which she practised a form of hierogamy. When her father heard of this, he ordered the

* It is a tenable theory that many of the goddesses of Greek mythology represent the fragmentation of a pre-Greek female figure in whose person their various functions were originally met.

[237]

statue to be burnt; but Laodamia proved her loyalty by immolating herself with it. (Poem 68)

LARISSA. A town in Thessaly on the River Peneus. (Poem 64)

LATIUM. A region of Italy. (Poem 57)

LATMOS. A mountain in Caria where Endymion was kept asleep by Diana. (Poem 66)

LATONA. (L.) The mother, by Jupiter, of Diana, to whom she gave birth leaning against an olive tree in Delos. (Poem 34)

LAVINIA. Vinia (*q.v.*).

LESBIA. Clodia Metelli (*q.v.*). (Poems 2, 3, 5, 7, 8, 11, 36, 43, 51, 58, 70, 72, 75, 76, 79, 83, 86, 87, 92, 107)

LIBO. An unidentified intimate of Caesar. (Poem 54)

LUCIFER. The light-bringer, the name by which Hesperus, the evening star, is known in the morning. (Poem 62)

MAENAD. A Bacchante, or female devotee of Bacchus; the term was also applied to the worshippers of Cybele. (Poems 63, 64)

MAGUS. A wise man or magician, particularly in reference to the Persians. (Poem 90)

MAMURRA. (L.) Caesar's chief engineer in Gaul, one of the dictator's intimates. He came from Formia in Latium. Hence, Catullus sometimes calls him 'Formianus'. (Poems 29, 57)

MANLIUS. L. Manlius Torquatus (*q.v.*). (Poems 61, 68)

MARCUS TULLIUS. (L.) Marcus Tullius Cicero (*q.v.*). (Poem 49)

MARS. (L.) The god of war, whom Vulcan, the lame blacksmith god, trapped under a net of fine-spun steel, while Mars was enjoying Vulcan's wife, Venus. (Poems, 17, 64)

MEGAERA. One of the three Furies (Poem 64)

MELLA. A river near Brescia. (Poem 67)

MEMMIUS. (L.) C. Memmius Gemellus, praetor in 58 B.C., governor of Bithynia in 57; a patron of Catullus whom he took with him to Bithynia. He was himself a poet of the new school. (Poems 10, 28)

MEMNON. King of Ethiopia, one of the sons of Aurora, the dawn. (Poem 66)

MENENIUS. Unidentified. (Poem 59)

MIDAS. (L.) The Phrygian King who turned all that he touched to gold. (Poem 24)

[238]

MINOA. A town in Crete. 'Minoan' is a synonym for 'Cretan', after Minos (L.), the first king. (Poem 64)

NASO. Unidentified. (Poem 112)

NAXOS. (L.) The largest of the Cyclades, where Bacchus was held in particular honour. It was the scene of Theseus's desertion of Ariadne and of her subsequent consolation by Bacchus. (Poem 64)

NEPOS. (L.) Cornelius Nepos, the historian, a friend of Cicero, possibly a Veronese. The *Carmina*, as we have it, is dedicated to him. It is not known whether all the references to 'Cornelius' are to the same person.

NEREIDS. (L.) The Nymphs of the Aegean sea. (Poems 64, 88)

NICAEA. A town in Bithynia. (Poem 46)

NONNIUS. Identification is uncertain, but we know that the curule aedileship for 54 B.C. was awarded to M. Nonnius Sufenas of Pompey's faction. (Poem 52)

OCEAN. (L.) Oceanus, the river-god, husband of Tethys; his waters girdled the earth. (Poems 64, 88)

OLYMPUS. (L.) The home of the gods. A mountain on the borders of Macedonia and Thessaly. (Poems 34, 64, 68)

ORCUS. Pluto, the god of the dead; hence, one of the names for the underworld. (Poem 3)

OREADS. The nymphs of caves and of mountains. (Poem 64)

O'TOOLE. Mamurra (*q.v.*). (Poems 94, 105, 114, 115)

OTTO. An unidentified intimate of Caesar. (Poem 54)

PANATHANAEA. (L.) The yearly sports held at Athens in honour of Athene. (Poem 64)

PARCAE. (L.) The three Fates, who weave the web of man's destiny. (Poem 64)

PARIS. (L.) One of the sons of Priam King of Troy, celebrated for his good looks. His elopement with Helen caused the Trojan War. (Poems 61, 68)

PARNASSUS. (L.) A mountain in Phocis sacred to Apollo and the Muses. (Poems 64, 105)

PARTHIA. A country in Asia, famous for its mounted archers. (Poem 11)

PASITHEA. One of the Graces, betrothed to the god of sleep. (Poem 63)

PEGASUS. (L.) The winged horse who, by stamping with his hoof, created the spring of Hippocrene on Mount Helicon. Hence, he represents the act of poetic creation. (Poem 55)

PELEUS. One of the Argonauts, King of Thessaly and grandson of Chiron the centaur. He was the only mortal to be awarded a goddess, Thetis, for a wife. (Poem 64)

PELION. (L.) A mountain in Thessaly. (Poem 64)

PENELOPE. (L.) Wife of Odysseus. She waited faithfully for twenty years for his return from Troy. (Poem 61)

PENEUS. (L.) A river in Thessaly. (Poem 64)

PERSEUS. (L.) The son of Jupiter and Danae. The winged sandals of Mercury were one of the gifts which the gods gave Perseus so that he could kill the Gorgon, Medusa. (Poem 55)

PESARO. A town on the Adriatic, in the Roman region of Umbria. It was low-lying and unhealthy. (Poem 81)

PHAETON. (L.) The son of Apollo. He was loved by Venus, a fact which made him so conceited that he tried to drive his father's chariot, but perished in the attempt. He fell to earth, landing in the River Po, since when his three sisters, Lampetrie, Phaetusa and Lampethusa, who are known as the Heliads, and are, in reality, the poplars which line the river banks, weep tears of amber for their lost brother. (Poem 64)

PHARSALIA. A plain in Thessaly named after the town of Pharsalus. (Poem 64)

PHRYGIA. (L.) A country in Asia Minor, noted for the worship of Cybele. (Poems 46, 63, 64)

PHTHIOTIC TEMPE. (L.) A beautiful valley in Thessaly situated between Olympus and Ossa. It is watered by the River Peneus. (Poem 64)

PIERIA. Traditionally regarded as the home of poetry. It was a district on the borders of Thessaly and Macedonia. (Poems 65, 68)

PIRAEUS. The harbour about three miles outside Athens. (Poem 64)

PISO. Traditionally, L. Calpurnius Piso Caesoninus, Caesar's father-in-law. (Poems 28, 47)

POLLIO. (L.) 'Pollionus' in the English translation. C. Asinius Pollio,

Supporter of Caesar and subsequently of the Triumvirate. He was a distinguished orator, patron and poet. (Poem 12)

POLLUX. (L.) One of the Dioscuri (*q.v.*). (Poems 4, 68)

POLYXENA. (L.) One of Priam's daughters. After the fall of Troy, she was sacrificed by Neoptolemus on his father's (Achilles's) tomb. (Poem 64)

POMPEY. (L.) Cn. Pompeius Magnus, contender with Julius Caesar for sole supremacy of the Roman world (poem 113). The battle of Pharsalia (48 B.C.) decided the issue in Caesar's favour. In 55 B.C. he opened a new *piazza* in the Campus Martius. This fact helps to date poem 55.

PONTIC SEA. The Black Sea. (Poems 4, 29)

POPLICOLA. L. Gellius Poplicola, presumably a rival for Clodia's favours. Later, in 36 B.C., he became consul. He fought for Antony at Actium.

PORCIUS. Unidentified. (Poem 47)

POSTUMIA. Unidentified. It was customary for a male member of a party to preside over the toasts, etc., but for a female most unusual, and suggests licentiousness. (Poem 27)

POSTUMIUS. Unidentified, presumably a Cisalpine. (Poem 67)

PRIAPUS. (L.) The god of gardens and of lust, the most prominent feature of whose statues was a disproportionately large phallus. (Poems 18, 47)

PROCNE. (L.) The wife of Tereus, King of Thrace. When her husband discovered the fate of their son, Itylus (*q.v.*), he tried to kill her, but the gods saved her by turning her into a swallow. (Poem 65)

PROMETHEUS. (L.) The Titan who stole fire – free will – from Heaven and gave it to mankind. Jupiter punished him by chaining him for thirty years to a rock in the Caucasus. Every day an eagle devoured his liver, and every night Jove provided him with a new one. He was finally released by Hercules. (Poem 64)

PROTESILAUS. (L.) The husband of Laodamia. It had been foretold that the first Greek to land at Troy would be killed as soon as he set foot on the beach. Protesilaus knew this, but was nevertheless the first to jump from the boats. (Poem 68)

PTOLEMY III. (L.) (246–221 B.C.), husband of Berenice. The two were cousins, the relationship of brother and sister, referred to in the text, being an erotic honorific, customary in ancient Egypt. (Poem 66)

PULCHER. P. Clodius Pulcher, a notorious associate of Caesar. He succeeded in driving Cicero abroad and then pillaging his house and goods. He profaned the Mysteries of the Mother Goddess by attending them dressed as a woman. He was also said to have committed incest with his sisters. (See in Lemprière under 'Clodius'.) (Poem 79)

QUINTIA. Unidentified. (Poem 86)
QUINTILIA. Either the wife, the mistress or the betrothed of C. Licinius Calvus. (Poem 96)
QUINTIUS. Unidentified. (Poems 82, 100)
QUINTUS. Unidentified. (Poem 67)

RAVIDUS. Unidentified; a rival for Clodia's favours. (Poem 40)
RHAMNUSIA. Another name for Nemesis or Fate. (Poem 68)
RHESUS. (L.) The King of Thrace whose horses were renowned for their speed. (Poem 55)
RIVER OF PHEASANTS. Phasis, a river in Colchis that rises in the Caucasus and empties into the Black Sea. It was the home of our European pheasants. (Poem 64)
RUFULUS. Unidentified. (Poem 59)
RUFUS. (L.) M. Caelius Rufus, a disciple of Cicero, who defended him against Clodius Pulcher's charges of involvement in the Cataline conspiracy. He was one of Clodia's lovers, but had broken with her by the time of the trial. As he is not known to have come from Cisalpine Gaul the Caelius of poem 100 cannot be referred to him with any certainty. (Poem 77)

SABINE. The Sabini were a neighbouring people who lived between the Nar and the Anio and were ultimately subdued by the Romans. The region near Tibur still preserved their name, but, unlike Tibur, did not provide a fashionable address. (Poems 39, 44)
SACIA. A country in Asia, bordering on the Caspian Sea. (Poem 11)
SAPPHO. (L.) The seventh-century Greek lyric poet (poem 35). Poem 51 is a direct translation of one of her poems. It marks the first known use of the Sapphic metre in Latin.

SATRACHUS. A city and river in Cyprus. (Poem 95)

SATURNALIA. (L.) The midwinter feast of Saturn. People gave each other presents; the shops closed, and an air of licence and merry-making prevailed. (Poem 14)

SATYRS. (L.) Demi-gods with the legs, hooves and horns of goats, who attended on Bacchus. (Poem 64)

SCAMANDER. (L.) One of the principal rivers of the Troad. (Poem 64)

SCYLLA. A twelve-necked monster on the Italian side of the Straits of Messina, opposite Charybdis, the whirlpool. (Poem 60)

SERAP. An Egyptian divinity whose temple stood in the suburbs of Rome. Serapis was identified by Apollodorus with the bull Apis, before whom women used to display themselves as a cure for sterility, and with whose priests they would, for similar purposes, have intercourse. The cult was ratified by Antoninus Pius in 146 A.D., but got out of hand and had to be suppressed. (Poem 10)

SESTIUS. P. Sestius, quaestor in 63 B.C., a close friend and colleague of Cicero. (Poem 44)

SIBYL. (L.) A prophetess of Apollo. The books of the most celebrated, the Cumaean Sibyl, were preserved on the Capitol. (Poem 77)

SILENES. (L.) Another word for Satyrs, and fauns generally. Silenus was a demi-god, Bacchus's principal attendant. (Poem 64)

SILO. Unidentified. (Poem 103)

SIMONIDES. (L.) The Greek lyric poet (556–467 B.C.). (Poem 38)

SIRMIO. The promontory on Lago di Garda where Catullus, or his father, owned a villa. (Poem 31)

SOCRATION. Unidentified. (Poem 47)

SPARTA. (L.) The capital of Laconia. Helen was the Queen of Sparta.

STYMPHALIA. From Stymphalus the name of a mountain, a town and a lake in Arcadia. It was the scene of Hercules's sixth labour, the slaughter of the man-eating stymphalides, monstrous birds who lived on an island in the lake. (Poem 68)

STYX. (L.) One of the rivers of the underworld. (Poem 65)

SUFFENUS. Unidentified, evidently a poet of the traditionalist school. (Poems 14, 22)

SUFFICIO. Unidentified intimate of Caesar. (Poem 54)

SULLA. Unidentified. (Poem 14)

SYRTES. (L.) Shoal water off the North African coast. (Poem 64)

TALASIUS. (L.) The Latin name for Hymen. (Poem 61)

TAPPO. Unidentified. (Poem 104)

TAURUS. A mountain in Asia Minor. (Poem 64)

TELEMACHUS. (L.) The son of Odysseus and Penelope. (Poem 61)

TETHYS. (L.) Sea goddess, wife of Oceanus. (Poems 64, 66, 88)

THALLUS. Unidentified. (Poem 25)

THEMIS. (L.) The goddess of Justice, traditionally depicted with scales and sword. She was the mother of the Parcae. (Poem 68)

THESEUS. (L.) Son of Aegeus King of Athens. He was brought up in Troezene. He sailed to Crete and slew the Minotaur, subsequently eloping with Ariadne whom he abandoned on Naxos – some say in favour of her sister, Phaedra. (Poem 64)

THESPIA. A town in Boeotia, near Mount Helicon. (Poem 61)

THETIS. (L.) A Nereid, wife of Peleus, by whom she bore Achilles. (Poem 64)

THIA. Another name for Macedonia. The Macedonians supported Xerxes' invasion of Greece, and the Ptolemaic dynasty, to whom the word is applied, were of Macedonian origin. (Poem 66)

THYIADES. Another name for Maenads, or Bacchantes, but especially applied to those of Delphos. (Poem 64)

THYNIA. A town in Bithynia. (Poem 31)

TIBUR. Modern Tivoli, a town on the Anio near Rome. It provided a fashionable country-address. (Poems 39, 44)

TISIPHONE. One of the three Furies. (Poem 64)

TORQUATUS. L. Manlius Torquatus, an orator and friend of Cicero. He was a supporter of Pompey; quaestor in 49 B.C.; killed in the Civil War, in North Africa in 47. (Poems 61, 68)

TROAD. The region round Troy. (Poem 68)

TROEZENE. A town in Argolis. Theseus was born and brought up there. (Poem 64)

TROY. A town near the Dardanelles. The scene of the Trojan War, which in Catullus symbolises the close of the age of the gods. (Poems 64, 68)

URANIA. (L.) One of the Muses, patron of astronomy. (Poem 61)

VARUS. P. Alfenus Varus, a Cremonese mentioned by Horace in his first satire as having given up a cobbler's shop for a career in the law courts. He was the first Cisalpine to attain the consulate. (Poems 10, 22)

VATINIUS. (L.) P. Vatinius, quaestor in 63 B.C., tribune in 59, praetor in 55 and consul in 47. He was a supporter of Caesar and a friend of Cicero. He was involved in several court cases in more than one of which Licinius Calvus was the prosecutor. On one occasion, when the case was going against him, Clodius and his henchmen forcibly broke up the proceedings. (Poems 14, 52, 53)

VENUS. (L.) Born of sea-foam. The wife of Vulcan, Mars's mistress, Cupid's mother. She is the goddess of elemental attraction. (Poems 3, 13, 29, 36, 45, 56, 61, 64, 66, 68, 86, 89)

VERANIUS. Also 'Veraniolus' in the English translation. Like Fabullus (q.v.), a close friend of Catullus. (Poems 12, 28, 47)

VESPER. Another name for Hesperus, or the planet Venus, which, in common with the moon, the sun and the other stars, was thought of as rising behind Mount Oeta in Thessaly. (Poem 62)

VIBENNIUS. Unidentified. (Poem 33)

VICTIUS. Unidentified. (Poem 98)

VINIA. The wife of L. Manlius Torquatus. Otherwise unidentified. (Poem 61)

VIRRO. Unidentified. (Poem 80)

VOLUSIUS. Unidentified. A long-winded poet, presumably contemporary with Catullus. (Poems 36, 95)

VULCAN (L.) The blacksmith god who married Venus. When he was born, his mother, Juno, threw him out of Heaven because he was so ugly. As a result, he broke his leg and has remained lame ever afterwards. At Jupiter's behest he made the first woman on earth, Pandora. He is celebrated for being the only person successfully to make a mockery of Love and War, heavy armour precluding the performance of one and rendering impotent the effects of the other. (Poem 36)

GLOSSARY

ZEPHYRUS. (L.) The West Wind, brother of Memnon, one of the sons of Aurora, the Dawn. (Poems 26, 46, 64)

ZERITHON. The local name for Pheneus, a town in Arcadia, with a lake of the same name. (Poem 68)

ZMYRNA. The title of a poem by C. Helvius Cinna, probably a miniature epic like the *Peleus and Thetis*. (Poem 95)

CATULLI CARMINA

I

Qvi dono lepidum nouum libellum
arido modo pumice expolitum?
Corneli, tibi: namque tu solebas
meas esse aliquid putare nugas;
iam tum cum ausus es unus Italorum
omne aeuum tribus explicare cartis
doctis, Iuppiter, et laboriosis.
quare habe tibi quidquid hoc libelli
qualecumque; quod, o patrona uirgo,
plus uno maneat perenne saeclo.

II

Passer, deliciae meae puellae,
quicum ludere, quem in sinu tenere,
qui primum digitum dare atpetenti
et acris solet incitare morsus,
cum desiderio meo nitenti
carum nescio quid libet iocari,
et solaciolum sui doloris,
†credo ut cum grauis acquiescet ardor:†
tecum ludere sicut ipsa possem
et tristis animi leuare curas!
. . . .
tam gratum est mihi quam ferunt puellae
pernici aureolum fuisse malum,
quod zonam soluit diu ligatam.

III

LVGETE, o Veneres Cupidinesque,
et quantum est hominum uenustiorum.
passer mortuus est meae puellae,
passer, deliciae meae puellae.
quem plus illa oculis suis amabat :
nam mellitus erat suamque norat
ipsam tam bene quam puella matrem.
nec sese a gremio illius mouebat,
sed circumsiliens modo huc modo illuc
ad solam dominam usque pipilabat.
qui nunc it per iter tenebricosum
illuc, unde negant redire quenquam.
at uobis male sit, malae tenebrae
Orci, quae omnia bella deuoratis :
tam bellum mihi passerem abstulistis.
uae factum male ! uae miselle passer,
tua nunc opera meae puellae
flendo turgiduli rubent ocelli.

IV

PHASELLVS ille, quem uidetis, hospites,
ait fuisse nauium celerrimus,
neque ullius natantis impetum trabis
nequisse praeterire, siue palmulis
opus foret uolare siue linteo.
et hoc negat minacis Adriatici
negare litus insulasue Cycladas
Rhodumque nobilem horridamque Thraciam,
Propontida trucemue Ponticum sinum,
ubi iste post phasellus antea fuit

comata silua : nam Cytorio in iugo
loquente saepe sibilum edidit coma.
Amastri Pontica et Cytore buxifer,
tibi haec fuisse et esse cognitissima
ait phasellus : ultima ex origine
tuo stetisse dicit in cacumine,
tuo imbuisse palmulas in aequore,
et inde tot per impotentia freta
herum tulisse, laeua siue dextera
uocaret aura, siue utrumque Iuppiter
simul secundus incidisset in pedem.
neque ulla uota litoralibus deis
sibi esse facta, cum ueniret a marei
nouissimo hunc ad usque limpidum lacum.
sed haec prius fuere : nunc recondita
senet quiete seque dedicat tibi,
gemelle Castor et gemelle Castoris.

V

Vivamvs, mea Lesbia, atque amemus,
rumoresque senum seueriorum
omnes unius aestimemus assis.
soles occidere et redire possunt :
nobis cum semel occidit breuis lux,
nox est perpetua una dormienda.
da mi basia mille, deinde centum,
dein mille altera, dein secunda centum,
deinde usque altera mille, deinde centum.
dein, cum milia multa fecerimus,
conturbabimus illa, ne sciamus,
aut ne quis malus inuidere possit,
cum tantum sciat esse basiorum.

[251]

VI

Flavi, delicias tuas Catullo,
nei sint illepidae atque inelegantes,
uelles dicere, nec tacere posses.
uerum nescio quid febriculosi
scorti diligis : hoc pudet fateri.
nam te non uiduas iacere noctes
nequiquam tacitum cubile clamat
Sertisque ac Syrio fraglans oliuo,
puluinusque peraeque et hic et ille
attritus, tremulique quassa lecti
argutatio inambulatioque.
nam nil uerpa ualet, nihil tacere.
cur? non tam latera ecfututa pandas,
nei tu quid facias ineptiarum.
quare, quidquid habes boni malique,
dic nobis. uolo te ac tuos amores
ad caelum lepido uocare uersu.

VII

Qvaeris, quot mihi basiationes
tuae, Lesbia, sint satis superque.
quam magnus numerus Libyssae harenae
lasarpiciferis iacet Cyrenis,
oraclum Iouis inter aestuosi
et Batti ueteris sacrum sepulcrum ;
aut quam sidera multa, cum tacet nox,
furtiuos hominum uident amores ;
tam te basia multa basiare
uesano satis et super Catullo est,
quae nec pernumerare curiosi
possint nec mala fascinare lingua.

VIII

MISER Catulle, desinas ineptire,
et quod uides perisse perditum ducas.
fulsere quondam candidi tibi soles,
cum uentitabas quo puella ducebat
amata nobis quantum amabitur nulla.
ibi illa multa tum iocosa fiebant,
quae tu uolebas nec puella nolebat.
fulsere uere candidi tibi soles.
nunc iam illa non uolt : tu quoque inpotens noli,
nec quae fugit sectare, nec miser uiue,
sed obstinata mente perfer, obdura.
uale, puella. iam Catullus obdurat,
nec te requiret nec rogabit inuitam.
at tu dolebis, cum rogaberis nulla.
scelesta †ne te†. quae tibi manet uita !
quis nunc te adibit ? cui uideberis bella ?
quem nunc amabis ? cuius esse diceris ?
quem basiabis ? cui labella mordebis ?
at tu, Catulle, destinatus obdura.

IX

VERANI, omnibus e meis amicis
antistans mihi milibus trecentis,
uenistine domum ad tuos Penates
fratresque unanimos anumque matrem ?
uenisti. o mihi nuntii beati !
uisam te incolumem audiamque Hiberum
narrantem loca, facta, nationes,

ut mos est tuus, applicansque collum
iucundum os oculosque suauiabor.
o quantum est hominum beatiorum,
quid me laetius est beatiusue?

X

VARVS me meus ad suos amores
uisum duxerat e foro otiosum,
scortillum, ut mihi tum repente uisum est,
non sane illepidum neque inuenustum.
huc ut uenimus, incidere nobis ʼ
sermones uarii, in quibus, quid esset
iam Bithynia, quo modo se haberet,
et quonam mihi profuisset aere.
respondi id quod erat, nihil neque ipsis
nec praetoribus esse nec cohorti,
cur quisquam caput unctius referret,
praesertim quibus esset irrumator
praetor, non faceret pili cohortem.
'at certe tamen,' inquiunt 'quod illic
natum dicitur esse, comparasti
ad lecticam hominis.' Ego, ut puellae
unum me facerem beatiorem,
'non' inquam 'mihi tam fuit maligne,
ut, prouincia quod mala incidisset,
non possem octo homines parare rectos.'
at mi nullus erat neque hic neque illic,
fractum qui ueteris pedem grabati
in collo sibi collocare posset.
hic illa, ut decuit cinaediorem,
'quaeso' inquit 'mihi, mi Catulle, paulum
istos †commoda: nam† uolo ad Sarapim

[254]

deferri.' ' mane? inquii puellae,
' istud quod modo dixeram me habere,
fugit me ratio : meus sodalis
Cinna est Gaius, is sibi parauit.
uerum, utrum illius an mei, quid ad me?
utor tam bene quam mihi pararim.
sed tu insulsa male et molesta uiuis,
per quam non licet esse neglegentem.'

XI

Fvri et Aureli, comites Catulli,
siue in extremos penetrabit Indos,
litus ut longe resonante Eoa
   tunditur unda,
siue in Hyrcanos Arabesque molles,
seu Sacas sagittiferosue Parthos,
siue quae septemgeminus colorat
   aequora Nilus,
siue trans altas gradietur Alpes,
Caesaris uisens monimenta magni,
Gallicum Rhenum †horribilesque ulti-
   mosque† Britannos,
omnia haec, quaecunque feret uoluntas
caelitum, temptare simul parati,
pauca nuntiate meae puellae
   non bona dicta.
cum suis uiuat ualeatque moechis,
quos simul complexa tenet trecentos,
nullum amans uere, sed identidem omnium
   ilia rumpens :
nec meum respectet, ut ante, amorem,
qui illius culpa cecidit uelut prati

ultimi flos, praetereunte postquam
   tactus aratro est.

XII

MARRVCINE Asini, manu sinistra
non belle uteris in ioco atque uino:
tollis lintea neglegentiorum.
hoc salsum esse putas? fugit te, inepte:
quamuis sordida res et inuenusta est.
non credis mihi? crede Pollioni
fratri, qui tua furta uel talento
mutari uelit: est enim leporum
disertus puer ac facetiarum.
quare aut hendecasyllabos trecentos
exspecta, aut mihi linteum remitte,
quod me non mouet aestimatione,
uerum est mnemosynum mei sodalis.
nam sudaria Saetaba ex Hiberis
miserunt mihi muneri Fabullus
et Veranius: haec amem necesse est
ut Veraniolum meum et Fabullum.

XIII

CENABIS bene, mi Fabulle, apud me
paucis, si tibi di fauent, diebus,
si tecum attuleris bonam atque magnam
cenam, non sine candida puella
et uino et sale et omnibus cachinnis.
haec si, inquam, attuleris, uenuste noster,
cenabis bene: nam tui Catulli
plenus sacculus est aranearum.
sed contra accipies meros amores

seu quid suauius elegantiusue est:
nam unguentum dabo, quod meae puellae
donarunt Veneres Cupidinesque,
quod tu cum olfacies, deos rogabis,
totum ut te faciant, Fabulle, nasum.

XIV

NEI te plus oculis meis amarem,
iucundissime Calue, munere isto
odissem te odio Vatiniano:
nam quid feci ego quidue sum locutus,
cur me tot male perderes poetis?
isti di mala multa dent clienti,
qui tantum tibi misit impiorum.
quod si, ut suspicor, hoc nouum ac repertum
munus dat tibi Sulla litterator,
non est mi male, sed bene ac beate,
quod non dispereunt tui labores.
di magni, horribilem et sacrum libellum!
quem tu scilicet ad tuum Catullum
misti, continuo ut die periret,
Saturnalibus, optimo dierum!
non non hoc tibi, salse, sic abibit.
nam, si luxerit, ad librariorum
curram scrinia, Caesios, Aquinos,
Suffenum, omnia colligam uenena,
ac te his suppliciis remunerabor.
uos hinc interea ualete abite
illuc, unde malum pedem attulistis,
saecli incommoda, pessimi poetae.

XV

COMMENDO tibi me ac meos amores,
Aureli. ueniam peto pudentem,
ut, si quicquam animo tuo cupisti,
quod castum expeteres et integellum,
conserues puerum mihi pudice,
non dico a populo : nihil ueremur
istos, qui in platea modo huc modo illuc
in re praetereunt sua occupati :
uerum a te metuo tuoque pene
infesto pueris bonis malisque.
quem tu qua lubet, ut lubet, moueto
quantum uis, ubi erit foris paratum :
hunc unum excipio, ut puto, pudenter.
quod si te mala mens furorque uecors
in tantam impulerit, sceleste, culpam,
ut nostrum insidiis caput lacessas ;
a tum te miserum malique fati,
quem attractis pedibus patente porta
percurrent raphanique mugilesque.

XVI

PEDICABO ego uos et irrumabo,
Aureli pathice et cinaede Furi,
qui me ex uersiculis meis putastis,
quod sunt molliculi, parum pudicum.
nam castum esse decet pium poetam
ipsum, uersiculos nihil necesse est,
qui tum denique habent salem ac leporem,
si sint molliculi ac parum pudici,
et quod pruriat incitare possint,
non dico pueris, sed his pilosis

qui duros nequeunt mouere lumbos.
uos, quod milia multa basiorum
legistis, male me marem putatis?
pedicabo ego uos et irrumabo.

XVII

O COLONIA, quae cupis ponte ludere longo,
et salire paratum habes, sed uereris inepta
crura ponticuli acsuleis stantis in rediuiuis,
ne supinus eat cauaque in palude recumbat;
sic tibi bonus ex tua pons libidine fiat,
in quo uel Salisubsali sacra suscipiantur:
munus hoc mihi maximi da, Colonia, risus.
quendam municipem meum de tuo uolo ponte
ire praecipitem in lutum per caputque pedesque,
uerum totius ut lacus putidaeque paludis
liuidissima maximeque est profunda uorago.
insulsissimus est homo, nec sapit pueri instar
bimuli tremula patris dormientis in ulna.
quoi cum sit uiridissimo nupta flore puella
et puella tenellulo delicatior haedo,
asseruanda nigerrimis diligentius uuis,
ludere hanc sinit ut lubet, nec pili facit uni,
nec se subleuat ex sua parte, sed uelut alnus
in fossa Liguri iacet suppernata securi,
tantundem omnia sentiens quam si nulla sit usquam.
talis iste meus stupor nil uidet, nihil audit,
ipse qui sit, utrum sit an non sit, id quoque nescit.
nunc eum uolo de tuo ponte mittere pronum,
si pote stolidum repente excitare ueternum;
et supinum animum in graui derelinquere caeno,
ferream ut soleam tenaci in uoragine mula.

XVIII

Hunc lucum tibi dedico consecroque, Priape,
qua domus tua Lampsaci est quaque   Priape.
nam te praecipue in suis urbibus colit ora
Hellespontia, ceteris ostriosior oris.

XXI

Avreli, pater esuritionum,
non harum modo, sed quot aut fuerunt
aut sunt aut aliis erunt in annis,
pedicare cupis meos amores.
nec clam : nam simul es, iocaris una,
haerens ad latus omnia experiris.
frustra : nam insidias mihi instruentem
tangam te prior irrumatione.
atqui si faceres satur, tacerem :
nunc ipsum id doleo, quod esurire
mellitus puer et sitire discet.
quare desine, dum licet pudico,
ne finem facias, sed irrumatus.

XXII

Svffenvs iste, Vare, quem probe nosti,
homo est uenustus et dicax et urbanus,
idemque longe plurimos facit uersus.
puto esse ego illi milia aut decem aut plura
perscripta, nec sic ut fit in palimpsesto
relata : cartae regiae, noui libri,
noui umbilici, lora rubra, membrana
derecta plumbo, et pumice omnia aequata.
haec cum legas tu, bellus ille et urbanus

Suffenus unus caprimulgus aut fossor
rursus uidetur : tantum abhorret ac mutat.
hoc quid putemus esse ? qui modo scurra
aut siquid hac re tersius uidebatur,
idem infaceto est infacetior rure,
simul poemata attigit, neque idem umquam
aeque est beatus ac poema cum scribit :
tam gaudet in se tamque se ipse miratur.
nimirum idem omnes fallimur, neque est quisquam
quem non in aliqua re uidere Suffenum
possis. suus cuique attributus est error :
sed non uidemus manticae quod in tergo est.

XXIII

FVREI, cui neque seruos est neque arca
nec cimex neque araneus neque ignis,
uerum est et pater et nouerca, quorum
dentes uel silicem comesse possunt,
est pulcre tibi cum tuo parente
et cum coniuge lignea parentis.
nec mirum : bene nam ualetis omnes,
pulcre concoquitis, nihil timetis,
non incendia, non graues ruinas,
non facta impia, non dolos ueneni,
non casus alios periculorum.
atqui corpora sicciora cornu
aut siquid magis aridum est habetis
sole et frigore et esuritione.
quare non tibi sit bene ac beate ?
a te sudor abest, abest saliua,
mucusque et mala pituita nasi.
hanc ad munditiem adde mundiorem,
quod culus tibi purior salillo est,

nec toto decies cacas in anno,
atque id durius est faba et lapillis,
quod tu si manibus teras fricesque,
non umquam digitum inquinare posses.
haec tu commoda tam beata, Furi,
noli spernere nec putare parui,
et sestertia quae soles precari
centum desine´: nam satis beatu's.

XXIV

O QVI flosculus es Iuuentiorum,
non horum modo, sed quot aut fuerunt
aut posthac aliis erunt in annis,
mallem diuitias Midae dedisses
isti, qui neque seruos est neque arca,
quam sic te sineres ab illo amari.
'qui? non est homo bellus?' inquies. est :
sed bello huic neque seruos est neque arca.
hoc tu quam lubet abice eleuaque :
nec seruom tamen ille habet neque arcam.

XXV

CINAEDE Thalle, mollior cuniculi capillo
uel anseris medullula uel imula oricilla
uel pene languido senis situque araneoso,
idemque, Thalle, turbida rapacior procella,
cum diua †mulier aries† ostendit oscitantes,
remitte pallium mihi meum, quod inuolasti,
sudariumque Saetabum catagraphosque Thynos,
inepte, quae palam soles habere tamquam auita.
quae nunc tuis ab ungŭibus reglutina et remitte,
ne laneum latusculum manusque mollicellas
inusta turpiter tibi flagella conscribillent,

et insolenter aestues, uelut minuta magno
deprensa nauis in mari, uesaniente uento.

XXVI

FVRI, uillula nostra non ad Austri
flatus opposita est neque ad Fauoni
nec saeui Boreae aut Apheliotae,
uerum ad milia quindecim et ducentos.
o uentum horribilem atque pestilentem!

XXVII

MINISTER uetuli puer Falerni
inger mi calices amariores,
ut lex Postumiae iubet magistrae
ebriosa acina ebriosioris.
at uos quo lubet hinc abite, lymphae,
uini pernicies, et ad seueros
migrate. hic merus est Thyonianus.

XXVIII

PISONIS comites, cohors inanis,
aptis sarcinulis et expeditis,
Verani optime tuque mi Fabulle,
quid rerum geritis? satisne cum isto
uappa frigoraque et famem tulistis?
ecquidnam in tabulis patet lucelli
expensum, ut mihi, qui meum secutus
praetorem refero datum lucello.
o Memmi, bene me ac diu supinum
tota ista trabe lentus irrumasti.
sed, quantum uideo, pari fuistis
casu: nam nihilo minore uerpa

farti estis.   pete nobiles amicos.
at uobis mala multa di deaeque
dent, opprobria Romulei Remique.

XXIX

Qvis hoc potest uidere, quis potest pati,
nisi impudicus et uorax et aleo,
Mamurram habere quod Comata Gallia
habebat uncti et ultima Britannia?
cinaede Romule haec uidebis et feres?
et ille nunc superbus et superfluens
perambulabit omnium cubilia,
ut albulus columbus aut Adoneus?
cinaede Romule haec uidebis et feres?
es impudicus et uorax et aleo.
eone nomine, imperator unice,
fuisti in ultima occidentis insula,
ut ista uostra diffututa mentula
ducenties comesset aut trecenties?
quid est alid sinistra liberalitas?
parum expatrauit an parum elluatus est?
paterna prima lancinata sunt bona ;
secunda praeda Pontica, inde tertia
Hibera, quam scit amnis aurifer Tagus.
†hunc Gallie timet et Britannie.†
quid hunc malum fouetis? aut quid hic potest
nisi uncta deuorare patrimonia?
eone nomine †urbis opulentissime†
socer generque, perdidistis omnia?

XXX

ALFENE immemor atque unanimis false sodalibus
iam te nil miseret, dure, tui dulcis amiculi?
iam me prodere, iam non dubitas fallere, perfide?
. . . .
. . . .
nec facta impia fallacum hominum caelicolis placent.
quae tu neglegis ac me miserum deseris in malis.
eheu quid faciant, dice, homines cuiue habeant fidem?
certe tute iubebas animam tradere, inique, me
inducens in amorem, quasi tuta omnia mi forent.
idem nunc retrahis te ac tua dicta omnia factaque
uentos irrita ferre ac nebulas aereas sinis.
si tu oblitus es, at di meminerunt, meminit Fides,
quae te ut paeniteat postmodo facti faciet tui.

XXXI

PAENE insularum, Sirmio, insularumque
ocelle, quascumque in liquentibus stagnis
marique uasto fert uterque Neptunus;
quam te libenter quamque laetus inuiso,
uix mi ipse credens Thuniam atque Bithunos
liquisse campos et uidere te in tuto.
o quid solutis est beatius curis?
cum mens onus reponit, ac peregrino
labore fessi uenimus larem ad nostrum,
desideratoque acquiescimus lecto.
hoc est quod unum est pro laboribus tantis.
salue o uenusta Sirmio atque hero gaude;
gaudete uosque o Lydiae lacus undae;
ridete quidquid est domi cachinnorum.

XXXII

AMABO, mea dulcis Ipsithilla,
meae deliciae, mei lepores,
iube ad te ueniam meridiatum.
et si iusseris, illud adiuuato,
ne quis liminis obseret tabellam,
neu tibi lubeat foras abire,
sed domi maneas paresque nobis
nouem continuas fututiones.
uerum si quid ages statim iubeto:
nam pransus iaceo et satur supinus
pertundo tunicamque palliumque.

XXXIII

O FVRVM optime balneariorum
Vibenni pater et cinaede fili,
(nam dextra pater inquinatiore,
culo filius est uoraciore)
cur non exilium malasque in oras
itis? quandoquidem patris rapinae
notae sunt populo, et natis pilosas,
fili, non potes asse uenditare.

XXXIV

DIANAE sumus in fide
    puellae et pueri integri:
    Dianam pueri integri
    puellaeque canamus.
o Latonia, maximi
    magna progenies Iouis,
    quam mater prope Deliam
    deposiuit oliuam,

montium domina ut fores
siluarumque uirentium
saltuumque reconditorum
amniumque sonantum :
tu Lucina dolentibus
Iuno dicta puerperis,
tu potens Triuia et notho's
dicta lumine Luna.
tu cursu, dea, menstruo
metiens iter annuum,
rustica agricolae bonis
tecta frugibus exples.
sis quocumque tibi placet
sancta nomine, Romulique
antique ut solita's bona
sospites ope gentem.

XXXV

POETAE tenero, meo sodali,
uelim Caecilio, papyre, dicas
Veronam ueniat, Noui relinquens
Comi moenia Lariumque litus.
nam quasdam uolo cogitationes
amici accipiat sui meique.
quare si sapiet uiam uorabit,
quamuis candida milies puella
euntem reuocet, manusque collo
ambas iniciens roget morari.
quae nunc, si mihi uera nuntiantur,
illum deperit impotente amore.
nam quo tempore legit incohatam
Dindymi dominam, ex eo misellae

ignes interiorem edunt medullam.
ignosco tibi, Sapphica puella
musa doctior; est enim uenuste
magna Caecilio incohata mater.

XXXVI

ANNALES Volusi, cacata carta,
uotum soluite pro mea puella.
nam sanctae Veneri Cupidinique
uouit, si sibi restitutus essem
desissemque truces uibrare iambos,
electissima pessimi poetae
scripta tardipedi deo daturam
infelicibus ustulanda lignis.
et haec pessima se puella uidit
iocose lepide uouere diuis.
nunc o caeruleo creata ponto,
quae sanctum Idalium Vriosque apertos,
quaeque Ancona Cnidumque harundinosam
colis quaeque Amathunta, quaeque Golgos,
quaeque Durrachium Hadriae tabernam;
acceptum face redditumque uotum,
si non illepidum neque inuenustum est.
at uos interea uenite in ignem,
pleni ruris et inficetiarum
annales Volusi, cacata carta.

XXXVII

Salax taberna uosque contubernales,
a pilleatis nona fratribus pila,
solis putatis esse mentulas uobis,
solis licere, quidquid est puellarum,
confutuere et putare ceteros hircos?
an, continenter quod sedetis insulsi
centum an ducenti, non putatis ausurum
me una ducentos irrumare sessores?
atqui putate: namque totius uobis
frontem tabernae †sopionibus† scribam.
puella nam mei, quae meo sinu fugit,
amata tantum quantum amabitur nulla,
pro qua mihi sunt magna bella pugnata,
consedit istic. hanc boni beatique
omnes amatis, et quidem, quod indignum est,
omnes pusilli et semitarii moechi;
tu praeter omnes une de capillatis,
cuniculosae Celtiberiae fili,
Egnati, opaca quem bonum facit barba
et dens Hibera defricatus urina.

XXXVIII

Malest, Cornifici, tuo Catullo,
malest, me hercule †et† laboriose,
et magis magis in dies et horas.
quem tu, quod minimum facillimumque est,
qua solatus es allocutione?
irascor tibi. sic meos amores?
paulum quid lubet allocutionis,
maestius lacrimis Simonideis.

XXXIX

EGNATIVS, quod candidos habet dentes,
renidet usque quaque : sei ad rei uentum est
subsellium, cum orator excitat fletum,
renidet ille : si ad pii rogum fili
lugetur, orba cum flet unicum mater,
renidet ille : quidquid est, ubicumque est,
quodcumque agit, renidet : hunc habet morbum,
neque elegantem, ut arbitror, neque urbanum.
quare monendum test mihi, bone Egnati.
si urbanus esses aut Sabinus aut Tiburs,
aut parcus Vmber aut obesus Etruscus,
aut Lanuinus ater atque dentatus,
aut Transpadanus, ut meos quoque attingam,
aut qui lubet, qui puriter lauit dentes,
tamen renidere usque quaque te nollem :
nam risu inepto res ineptior nulla est.
nunc Celtiber es : Celtiberia in terra,
quod quisque minxit, hoc sibi solet mane
dentem atque russam defricare gingiuam,
ut quo iste uester expolitior dens est,
hoc te amplius bibisse praedicet loti.

XL

QVAENAM te mala mens, miselle Rauide,
agit praecipitem in meos iambos?
quis- deus tibi non bene aduocatus
uecordem parat excitare rixam?
an ut peruenias in ora uulgi?
quid uis? qua lubet esse notus optas?
eris, quandoquidem meos amores
cum longa uoluisti amare poena.

XLI

AMEANA puella defututa
tota milia me decem poposcit,
ista turpiculo puella naso,
decoctoris amica Formiani.
propinqui, quibus est puella curae,
amicos medicosque conuocate:
non est sana puella, nec rogare
qualis sit solet aes imaginosum.

XLII

ADESTE, hendecasyllabi, quot estis
omnes undique, quotquòt estis omnes.
iocum me putat esse moecha turpis,
et negat mihi uestra reddituram
pugillaria, si pati potestis.
persequamur eam, et reflagitemus.
quae sit, quaeritis. illa, quam uidetis
turpe incedere, mimice ac moleste
ridentem catuli ore Gallicani.
circumsistite eam, et reflagitate,
' moecha putida, redde codicillos,
redde, putida moecha, codicillos.'
non assis facis? o lutum, lupanar,
aut si perditius potes quid esse.
sed non est tamen hoc satis putandum.
quod si non aliud potest, ruborem
ferreo canis exprimamus ore.
conclamate iterum altiore uoce
' moecha putida, redde codicillos,
redde, putida moecha codicillos,'

sed nil proficimus, nihil mouetur.
mutanda est ratio modusque uobis,
siquid proficere amplius potestis,
'pudica et proba, redde codicillos.'

XLIII

SALVE, nec minimo puella naso,
nec bello pede nec nigris ocellis,
nec longis digitis nec ore sicco,
nec sane nimis elegante lingua,
decoctoris amica Formiani.
ten prouincia narrat esse bellam?
tecum Lesbia nostra comparatur?
o saeclum insapiens et infacetum!

XLIV

O FVNDE noster seu Sabine seu Tiburs,
(nam te esse Tiburtem autumant, quibus non est
cordi Catullum laedere : at quibus cordi est,
quouis Sabinum pignore esse contendunt)
sed seu Sabine siue uerius Tiburs,
fui libenter in tua suburbana
uilla, malamque pectore exspui tussim,
non inmerenti quam mihi meus uenter,
dum sumptuosas appeto, dedit, cenas.
nam, Sestianus dum uolo esse conuiua,
orationem in Antium petitorem
plenam ueneni et pestilentiae legi.
hic me grauedo frigida et frequens tussis
quassauit usque dum in tuum sinum fugi,
et me recuraui otioque et urtica.
quare refectus maximas tibi grates

ago, meum quod non es ulta peccatum.
nec deprecor iam, si nefaria scripta
Sesti recepso, quin grauedinem et tussim
non mihi, sed ipsi Sestio ferat frigus,
qui tunc uocat me, cum malum librum legi.

XLV

ACMEN Septimios suos amores
tenens in gremio 'mea' inquit 'Acme,
ni te perdite amo atque amare porro
omnes sum assidue paratus annos
quantum qui pote plurimum perire,
solus in Libya Indiaque tosta
caesio ueniam obuius leoni.'
hoc ut dixit, Amor sinistra ut ante,
dextram sternuit approbationem.
at Acme leuiter caput reflectens,
et dulcis pueri ebrios ocellos
illo purpureo ore suauiata,
'sic,' inquit 'mea uita Septimille,
huic uni domino usque seruiamus,
ut multo mihi maior acriorque
ignis mollibus ardet in medullis.'
hoc ut dixit, Amor sinistra ut ante,
dextram sternuit approbationem.
nunc ab auspicio bono profecti
mutuis animis amant amantur.
unam Septimios misellus Acmen
mauúlt quam Syrias Britanniasque:
uno in Septimio fidelis Acme
facit delicias libidinisque.
quis ullos homines beatiores
uidit, quis Venerem auspicatiorem?

XLVI

IAM uer egelidos refert tepores,
iam caeli furor aequinoctialis
iucundis Zephyri silescit aureis.
linquantur Phrygii, Catulle, campi
Nicaeaeque ager uber aestuosae:
ad claras Asiae uolemus urbes.
iam mens praetrepidans auet uagari,
iam laeti studio pedes uigescunt.
o dulces comitum ualete coetus,
longe quos simul a domo profectos
diuersae uariae uiae reportant.

XLVII

PORCI et Socration, duae sinistrae
Pisonis, scabies famesque mundi,
uos Veraniolo meo et Fabullo
uerpus praeposuit Priapus ille?
uos conuiuia lauta sumptuose
de die facitis? mei sodales
quaerunt in triuio uocationes?

XLVIII

MELLITOS oculos tuos, Iuuenti,
siquis me sinat usque basiare,
usque ad milia basiem trecenta,
nec *mi* umquam uidear satur futurus,
non si densior aridis aristis
sit nostrae seges osculationis.

XLIX

DISERTISSIME Romuli nepotum,
quot sunt quotque fuere, Marce Tulli,
quotque post aliis erunt in annis,
gratias tibi maximas Catullus
agit pessimus omnium poeta,
tanto pessimus omnium poeta,
quanto tu optimus omnium's patronum.

L

HESTERNO, Licini, die. otiosi
multum lusimus in meis tabellis,
ut conuenerat esse delicatos.
scribens uersiculos uterque nostrum
ludebat numero modo hoc modo illoc,
reddens mutua per iocum atque uinum.
atque illinc abii tuo lepore
incensus, Licini, facetieisque,
ut nec me miserum cibus iuuaret,
nec somnus tegeret quiete ocellos,
sed toto indomitus furore lecto
uersarer, cupiens uidere lucem,
ut tecum loquerer, simulque ut essem.
at defessa labore membra postquam
semimortua lectulo iacebant,
hoc, iucunde, tibi poema feci,
ex quo perspiceres meum dolorem.
nunc audax caue sis, precesque nostras,
oramus, caue despuas, ocelle,
ne poenas Nemesis reposcat a te.
est uehemens dea : laedere hanc caueto.

LI

ILLE mi par esse deo uidetur,
ille, si fas est, superare diuos,
qui sedens aduersus identidem te
    spectat et audit
dulce ridentem, misero quod omnis
eripit sensus mihi: nam simul te,
Lesbia, aspexi, nihil est super mi
    . . . .
lingua sed torpet, tenuis sub artus
flamma demanat, sonitu suopte
tintinant aures, gemina teguntur
    lumina nocte.
            *
otium, Catulle, tibi molestum est:
otio exsultas nimiumque gestis:
otium et reges prius et beatas
    perdidit urbes.

LII

QVID est, Catulle? quid moraris emori?
sella in curulei Struma Nonius sedet,
per consulatum perierat Vatinius:
quid est, Catulle? quid moraris emori?

LIII

RISI nescio quem modo e corona,
qui, cum mirifice Vatiniana
meus crimina Caluos explicasset,
admirans ait haec manusque tollens,
'di magni, salaputium disertum!'

[276]

LIV

OTHONIS caput oppido est pusillum,
†et Heri† rustice, semilauta crura,
subtile et leue peditum Libonis.

. . . .

. . . .

at non effugies meos iambos

. . . .

. . . .

si non omnia displicere uellem
·tibi et Fufficio seni recocto

. . . .

irascere iterum meis iambis
inmerentibus, unice imperator.

LV

ORAMVS, si forte non molestum est,
demonstres ubi sint tuae tenebrae.
te campo quaesiuimus minore,
te in Circo, te in omnibus libellis,
te in templo summi Iouis sacrato.
in Magni simul ambulatione
femellas omnes, amice, prendi,
quas uultu uidi tamen serenas.
†a uelte†, sic ipse flagitabam,
Camerium mihi pessimae puellae.
quaedam inquit, nudum reduc . . .
' en hic in roseis latet papillis.'
sed te iam ferre Herculei labos est;
tanto te in fastu negas, amice.

non custos si fingar ille Cretum,
non si Pegaseo ferar uolatu,
non Ladas ego pinnipesue Perseus,
non Rhesi niueae citaeque bigae ;
adde huc plumipedas uolatilesque,
uentorumque simul require cursum,
quos iunctos, Cameri, mihi dicares ;
defessus tamen omnibus medullis,
et multis languoribus peresus,
essem te mihi, amice, quaeritando.
dic nobis ubi sis futurus, ede
audacter, committe, crede lucei.
nunc te lacteolae tenent puellae ?
si linguam clauso tenes in ore,
fructus proicies amoris omnes.
uerbosa gaudet Venus loquella.
uel, si uis, licet obseres palatum,
dum nostri sis particeps amoris.

LVI

O REM ridiculam, Cato, et iocosam,
dignamque auribus et tuo cachinno.
ride, quidquid amas, Cato, Catullum :
res est ridicula et nimis iocosa.
deprendi modo pupulum puellae
trusantem : hunc ego, si placet Dionae,
protelo rigida mea cecidi.

LVII

Pvlcre conuenit improbis cinaedis,
Mamurrae pathicoque Caesarique.
nec mirum : maculae paris utrisque,
urbana altera et illa Formiana,
impressae resident nec eluentur :
morbosi pariter, gemelli utrique,
uno in lectulo, erudituli ambo,
non hic quam ille magis uorax adulter,
riuales sociei puellularum.
pulcre conuenit improbis cinaedis.

LVIII

Caeli, Lesbia nostra, Lesbia illa,
illa Lesbia, quam Catullus unam
plus quam se atque suos amauit omnes,
nunc in quadruuiis et angiportis
glubit magnanimis Remi nepotes.

LIX

Bononiensis Rufa Rufulum fellat,
uxor Meneni, saepe quam in sepulcretis
uidistis ipso rapere de rogo cenam,
cum deuolutum ex igne prosequens panem
ab semiraso tunderetur ustore.

LX

Nvm te leaena montibus Libystinis
aut Scylla latrans infima inguinum parte
tam mente dura procreauit ac taetra,
ut supplicis uocem in nouissimo casu
contemptam haberes, a nimis fero corde?

LXI

COLLIS o Heliconiei
cultor, Vraniae genus,
qui rapis teneram ad uirum
Virginem, o Hymenaee Hymen,
Hymen o Hymenaee;

Cinge tempora floribus
suaue olentis amaraci,
flammeum cape laetus, huc
Huc ueni, niueo gerens
luteum pede soccum.

Excitusque hilari die,
nuptialia concinens
uoce carmina tinnula,
Pelle humum pedibus, manu
pineam quate taedam.

Namque Iunia Mallio,
qualis Idalium colens
uenit ad Phrygium Venus
Iudicem, bona cum bona
nubet alite uirgo,

Floridis uelut enitens
myrtus Asia ramulis
quos Amadryades deae
Ludicrum sibi rosido
nutriunt umore.
Quare age, huc aditum ferens,
perge linquere Thespiae
rupis Aonios specus,

Nympha quos super irrigat
frigerans Aganippe.

Ac domum dominam uoca
coniugis cupidam noui,
mentem amore reuinciens
Vt tenax hedera huc et huc
arborem implicat errans.

Vosque item simul integrae
uirgines, quibus aduenit
par dies, agite in modum
Dicite, O Hymenaee Hymen,
Hymen O Hymenaee.

Vt lubentius, audiens
se citarier ad suum
munus, huc aditum ferat
Dux bonae Veneris, boni
coniugator amoris.

Quis deus magis ancsiis
est petendus amantibus?
quem colent homines magis
Caelitum, O Hymenaee Hymen,
Hymen O Hymenaee?

Te suis tremulus parens
inuocat, tibi uirgines
zonula soluunt sinus.
Te timens cupida nouos
captat aure maritus.

[281]

Tu fero iuueni in manus
floridam ipse puellulam
dedis a gremio suae
Matris, O Hymenaee Hymen,
Hymen O Hymenaee.

Nil potest sine te Venus,
fama quod bona comprobet,
commodi capere, at potest
Te uolente. quis huic deo
compararier ausit?

Nulla quit sine te domus
liberos dare, nec parens
stirpe nitier; at potest
Te uolente. quis huic deo
compararier ausit?

Quae tuis careat sacris,
non queat dare praesides
terra finibus: at queat
Te uolente. quis huic deo
compararier ausit?

Claustra pandite ianuae.
uirgo adest. uiden ut faces
splendidas quatiunt comas?
. . . .
. . . .
. . . .
. . . .
tardet ingenuus pudor.
Quem tamen magis audiens,
flet quod ire necesse est.

Flere desine. non tibi Aurunculeia periculum est,
 ne qua femina pulcrior
Clarum ab Oceano diem
 uiderit uenientem.

Talis in uario solet
 diuitis domini hortulo
 stare flos hyacinthinus.
Sed moraris, abit dies.
 prodeas noua nupta.

Prodeas noua nupta, si
 iam uidetur, et audias
 nostra uerba. uiden? faces
Aureas quatiunt. comas :
 prodeas noua nupta.

Non tuus leuis in mala
 deditus uir adultera,
 probra turpia persequens,
A tuis teneris uolet
 secubare papillis.

Lenta qui uelut adsitas
 uitis implicat arbores,
 implicabitur in tuum
Complexum. sed abit dies.
 prodeas noua nupta.

O cubile, quod omnibus
 . . ` . . . . .
 . . . .
 . . . .
 candido pede lecti,

Quae tuo ueniunt hero,
  quanta gaudia, quae uaga
  nocte, quae medio die
Gaudeat. sed abit dies.
  prodeas noua .nupta.

Tollite, O pueri, faces.
  flammeum uideo uenire.
  ite concinite in modum
'Io Hymen Hymenaee io,
  io Hymen Hymenaee.'

Ne diu taceat procax
  Fescennina iocatio.
  nec nuces pueris neget
Desertum domini audiens
  concubinus amorem.

Da nuces pueris, iners
  concubine : satis diu
  lusisti nucibus. lubet
Iam seruire Talasio.
  concubine, nuces ḍa.

Sordebant tibi uillicae,
  concubine, hodie atque heri.
  nunc tuum cinerarius
Tondet os. miser a miser
  concubine, nuces da.

Diceris male te a tuis
  unguentate glabris marite
  abstinere, sed abstine.
Io Hymen Hymenaee io,
  io Hymen Hymenaee.

[284]

Scimus haec tibi quae licent
sola cognita, sed marito
ista non eadem licent.
Io Hymen Hymenaee io,
io Hymen Hymenaee.

Nupta, tu quoque quae tuus
uir petet caue ne neges,
ni petitum aliunde eat.
Io Hymen Hymenaee io,
io Hymen Hymenaee.

En tibi domus ut potens
et beata uiri tui.
quae tibi sine seruiat
(Io Hymen Hymenaee io,
io Hymen Hymenaee)

Vsque dum tremulùm mouens
cana tempus anilitas
omnia omnibus annuit.
Io Hymen Hymenaee io,
io Hymen Hymenaee.

Transfer omine cum bono
limen aureolos pedes,
rasilemque subi forem.
Io Hymen Hymenaee io,
io Hymen Hymenaee.
Aspice unus ut accubans
uir tuus Tyrio in toro,
totus immineat tibi.
Io Hymen Hymenaee io,
io Hymen Hymenaee.

Illi non minus ac tibi
 pectore uritur intimo
 flamma, sed penite magis.
Io Hymen Hymenaee io,
 io Hymen Hymenaee.

. . . .

 . . . .

 . . . .

. . . .

 . . . .

Mitte brachiolum teres,
 praetextate, puellulae.
 iam cubile adeat uiri.
Io Hymen Hymenaee io,
 io Hymen Hymenaee.

Vos bonae senibus uiris
 cognitae bene feminae,
 collocate puellulam.
Io Hymen Hymenaee io,
 io Hymen Hymenaee.

Iam licet uenias, marite.
 uxor in thalamo tibi est,
 ore floridulo nitens
Alba parthenice uelut
 luteumue papauer.

At, marite, ita me iuuent
 caelites, nihilo minus
 pulcer es, neque te Venus
Neglegit. sed abit dies.
 perge ne remorare.

Non diu remoratus es.
   iam uenis. bona te Venus
   iuuerit, quoniam palam
Quae cupis capis et bonum
   non abscondis amorem.

Ille pulueris Africei
   siderumque micantium
   subducat numerum prius,
Qui uostri numerare uolt
   multa milia ludei.

Ludite ut lubet et breui
   liberos date. non decet
   tam uetus sine liberis
Nomen esse, sed indidem
   semper ingenerari.

Torquatus uolo paruulus
   matris e gremio suae
   porrigens teneras manus,
Dulce rideat ad patrem
   semihiante labello.

Sit suo similis patri
   Mallio et facile inscieis
   noscitetur ab omnibus,
Et pudicitiam suo
   matris indicet ore.

Talis illius a bona
   matre laus genus approbet,
   qualis unica ab optima
Matre Telemacho manet
   fama Penelopeo.

Claudite ostia uirgines.
lusimus satis. at bonei
coniuges, bene uiuite et
Munere assidue ualentem
exercete iuuentam.

LXII

IVVENES

VESPER adest, iuuenes, consurgite : Vesper Olympo
exspectata diu uix tandem lumina tollit.
surgere iam tempus, iam pinguis linquere mensas,
iam ueniet uirgo, iam dicetur hymenaeus.
Hymen O Hymenaee, Hymen ades O Hymenaee!

VIRGINES

Cernitis, innuptae, iuuenes? consurgite contra ;
nimirum Oetaeos ostendit noctifer ignes.
sic certest ; uiden ut perniciter exsiluere?
non temere exsiluere, canent quod uisere par est.
Hymen O Hymenaee, Hymen ades O Hymenaee!

IVVENES

Non facilis nobis, aequalis, palma parata est,
aspicite, innuptae secum ut meditata requirunt.
non frustra meditantur, habent memorabile quod sit,
nec mirum, penitus quae tota mente laborant.
nos alio mentes, alio diuisimus aures,
iure igitur uincemur, amat uictoria curam.
quare nunc animos saltem committite uestros,
dicere iam incipient, iam respondere decebit.
Hymen O Hymenaee, Hymen ades O Hymenaee.

VIRGINES

Hespere, qui caelo fertur crudelior ignis?
qui natam possis complexu auellere matris,
complexu matris retinentem auellere natam,
et iuueni ardenti castam donare puellam.
quid faciunt hostes capta crudelius urbe?
Hymen O Hymenaee, Hymen ades O Hymenaee!

IVVENES

Hespere, qui caelo lucet iucundior ignis?
qui desponsa tua firmes conubia flamma,
quae pepigere uiri, pepigerunt ante parentes,
nec iunxere prius quam se tuus extulit ardor.
quid datur a diuis felici optatius hora?
Hymen O Hymenaee, Hymen ades O Hymenaee!

VIRGINES

Hesperus e nobis, aequalis, abstulit unam.
. . . .
. . . .
. . . . ,
. . . .
. . . .
. . . .
[Hymen O Hymenaee, Hymen ades O Hymenaee!]

IVVENES

. . . .
. . . .
Namque tuo aduentu uigilat custodia semper,
nocte latent fures, quos idem saepe reuertens,
Hespere, mutato comprendis nomine eosdem.
at libet innuptis ficto te carpere questu.
quid tum, si carpunt, tacita quem mente requirunt?
Hymen O Hymenaee, Hymen ades O Hymenaee!

VIRGINES

Vt flos in saeptis secretus nascitur hortis,
ignotus pecori, nullo contusus aratro,
quem mulcent aurae, firmat sol, educat imber;
multi illum pueri, multae optauere puellae:
idem cum tenui carptus defloruit ungui,
nulli illum pueri, nullae optauere puellae:
sic uirgo, dum intacta manet, dum cara suis est;
cum castum amisit polluto corpore florem,
nec pueris iucunda manet, nec cara puellis.
Hymen o Hymenaee, Hymen ades o Hymenaee!

IVVENES

Vt uidua in nudo uitis quae nascitur aruo,
numquam se extollit, numquam mitem educat uuam,
sed tenerum prono deflectens pondere corpus,
iam iam contingit summum radice flagellum,
hanc nulli agricolae, nulli coluere iuuenci:
at si forte eadem est ulmo coniuncta marito,
multi illam agricolae, multi accoluere iuuenci:
sic uirgo dum intacta manet, dum inculta senescit;
cum par conubium maturo tempore adepta est,
cara uiro magis et minus est inuisa parenti.

et tu ne pugna cum tali coniuge uirgo,
non aequom est pugnare, pater cui tradidit ipse.
ipse pater cum matre, quibus parere necesse est.
. . . .
uirginitas non tota tua est, ex parte parentum est,
tertia pars patrist, pars est data tertia matri,
tertia sola tua est: noli pugnare duobus,
qui genero sua iura simul cum dote dederunt.
Hymen o Hymenaee, Hymen ades o Hymenaee!

LXIII

SVPER alta uectus Attis celeri rate maria,
Phrygium ut nemus citato cupide pede tetigit,
adiitque opaca siluis redimita loca deae,
stimulatus ibi furenti rabie, uagus animis,
deuoluit ile acuto sibi pondere silicis.
itaque ut relicta sensit sibi membra sine uiro,
etiam recente terrae sola sanguine maculans,
niueis citata cepit manibus leue typanum,
typanum, tubam Cybelles, tua, mater, initia,
quatiensque terga taurei teneris caua digitis,
canere haec suis adorta est tremebunda comitibus.
agite ite ad alta, Gallae, Cybeles nemora simul,
simul ite, Dindimenae dominae 'uaga pecora,
aliena quae petentes uelut exules loca,
sectam meam exsecutae duce me mihi comites,
rapidum salum tulistis truculentaque pelagi,
et corpus euirastis Veneris nimio odio;
hilarate aere citatis erroribus animum.
mora tarda mente cedat: simul ite, sequimini
Phrygiam ad domum Cybelles, Phrygia ad nemora deae,
ubi cymbalum sonat uox, ubi tympana reboant,
tibicen ubi canit Phryx curuo graue calamo,
ubi capita Maenades ui iaciunt hederigerae,
ubi sacra sancta acutis ululatibus agitant,
ubi sueuit illa diuae uolitare uaga cohors,
quo nos decet citatis celerare tripudiis.
simul haec comitibus Attis cecinit notha mulier,
thiasus repente linguis trepidantibus ululat,
leue tympanum remugit, caua cymbala recrepant,
uiridem citus adit Idam properante pede chorus.
furibunda simul anhelans uaga uadit animam agens

comitata tympano Attis per opaca nemora dux,
ueluti iuuenca uitans onus indomita iugi :
rapidae ducem secuntur Gallae properipedem.
itaque, ut domum Cybelles tetigere lassulae,
nimio e labore somnum capiunt sine Cerere.
piger his labante languore oculos sopor operit :
abit in quiete molli rabidus furor animi.
sed ubi oris aurei Sol radiantibus oculis
lustrauit aethera album, sola dura, mare ferum,
pepulitque noctis umbras uegetis sonipedibus,
ibi Somnus excitum Attin fugiens citus abiit :
trepidante eum recepit dea Pasithea sinu.
ita de quiete molli rapida sine rabie
simul ipse pectore Attis sua facta recoluit,
liquidaque mente uidit sine queis ubique foret,
animo aestuante rusum reditum ad uada tetulit.
ibi maria uasta uisens lacrimantibus oculis,
patriam allocuta maestast ita uoce miseriter.
'patria o mei creatrix, patria o mea genetrix,
ego quam miser relinquens, dominos ut herifugae
famuli solent, ad Idae tetuli nemora pedem,
ut aput niuem et ferarum gelida stabula forem,
et earum omnia adirem furibunda latibula,
ubinam aut quibus locis te positam, patria, reor ?
cupit ipsa pupula ad te sibi dirigere aciem,
rabie fera carens dum breue tempus animus est.
egone a mea remota haec ferar in nemora domo ?
patria, bonis, amicis, genitoribus abero ?
abero foro, palaestra, stadio et gymnasiis ?
miser a miser, querendum est etiam atque etiam, anime.
quod enim genus figuraest, ego non quod obierim ?
ego mulier, ego adolescens, ego ephebus, ego puer,

ego gymnasei fui flos, ego eram decus olei:
mihi ianuae frequentes, mihi limina tepida,
mihi floridis corollis redimita domus erat,
linquendum ubi esset orto mihi Sole cubiculum.
ego nunc deum ministra et Cybeles famula ferar?
ego Maenas, ego mei pars, ego uir sterilis ero?
ego uiridis algida Idae niue amicta loca cŏlam?
ego uitam agam sub altis Phrygiae columinibus,
ubi cerua siluicultrix, ubi aper nemoriuagus?
iam iam dolet quod egi, iam iamque paenitet.'
roseis ut huic labellis sonitus citus abiit,
geminas deorum ad auris noua nuntia referens,
ibi iuncta iuga resoluens Cybele leonibus
laeuumque pecoris hostem stimulans ita loquitur.
'agedum' inquit 'age ferox i, face ut hunc furor agitet,
face uti furoris ictu reditum in nemora ferat,
mea libere nimis qui fugere imperia cupit.
age caede terga cauda, tua uerbera patere,
face cuncta mugienti fremitu loca retonent,
rutilam ferox torosa ceruice quate iubam.'
ait haec minax Cybelle religatque iuga manu.
ferus ipse sese adhortans rapidum incitat animo,
uadit, fremit, refringit uirgulta pede uago.
at ubi umida albicantis loca litoris adiit,
tenerumque uidit Attin prope marmora pelagei,
facit impetum: ille demens fugit in nemora fera:
ibi semper omne uitae spatium famula fuit.
dea, magna dea, Cybelle, dea, domina Dindimei,
procul a mea tuos sit furor omnis, hera, domo:
alios age incitatos, alios age rabidos.

LXIV

PELIACO quondam prognatae uertice pinus
dicuntur liquidas Neptuni nasse per undas
Phasidos ad fluctus et fines Aeetaeos,
cum lecti iuuenes, Argiuae robora pubis,
auratam optantes Colchis auertere pellem
ausi sunt uada salsa cita decurrere puppi,
caerula uerrentes abiegnis aequora palmis.
diua quibus retinens in summis urbibus arces,
ipsa leui fecit uolitantem flamine currum,
pinea coniungens inflexae texta carinae.
illa rudem cursu prima imbuit Amphitriten.
quae simul ac rostro uentosum proscidit aequor,
tortaque remigio spumis incanuit unda,
emersere feri candenti e gurgite uultus
aequoreae monstrum Nereides admirantes.
illa, atque haud alia, uiderunt luce marinas
mortales oculi nudato corpore Nymphas
nutricum tenus exstantes e gurgite cano.
tum Thetidis Peleus incensus fertur amore,
tum Thetis humanos non despexit hymenaeos,
tum Thetidi pater ipse iugandum Pelea sensit.
o nimis optato saeclorum tempore nati
heroes, saluete, deum genus! o bona mater!
uos ego saepe meo uos carmine compellabo.
teque adeo eximie taedis felicibus aucte,
Thessaliae columen Peleu, cui Iuppiter ipse,
ipse suos diuum genitor concessit amores.
tene Thetis tenuit pulcerrima Neptunine?
tene suam Tethys concessit ducere neptem,
Oceanusque, mari totum qui amplectitur orbem?
quae simul optato finitae tempore luces

aduenere, domum conuentu tota frequentat
Thessalia, oppletur laetanti regia coetu:
dona ferunt prae se, declarant gaudia uultu.
deseritur Scyros, linquunt Phthiotica Tempe,
Crannonisque domos ac moenia Larisaea,
Pharsaliam coeunt, Pharsalia tecta frequentant.
rura colit nemo, mollescunt colla iuuencis,
non humilis curuis purgatur uinea rastris,
non glebam prono conuellit uomere taurus,
non falx attenuat frondatorum arboris umbram,
squalida desertis rubigo infertur aratris.
ipsius at sedes, quacumque opulenta recessit
regia, fulgenti splendent auro atque argento.
candet ebur soliis, collucent pocula mensae,
tota domus gaudet regali splendida gaza.
puluinar uero diuae geniale locatur
sedibus in mediis, Indo quod dente politum
tincta tegit roseo conchyli purpura fuco.
haec uestis priscis hominum uariata figuris
heroum mira uirtutes indicat arte.
namque fluentisono prospectans litore Diae,
Thesea cedentem celeri cum classe tuetur
indomitos in corde gerens Ariadna furores,
necdum etiam sese quae uisit uisere credit,
ut pote fallaci quae tum primum excita somno
desertam in sola miseram se cernat harena.
immemor at iuuenis fugiens pellit uada remis,
irrita uentosae linquens promissa procellae.
quem procul ex alga maestis Minois ocellis,
saxea ut effigies bacchantis, prospicit, eheu,
prospicit et magnis curarum fluctuat undis,
non flauo retinens subtilem uertice mitram,
non contecta leui uelatum pectus amictu,

non tereti strophio lactentis uincta papillas,
omnia quae toto delapsa e corpore passim
ipsius ante pedes fluctus salis alludebant.
sed neque tum mitrae neque tum fluitantis amictus
illa uicem curans toto ex te pectore, Theseu,
toto animo, tota pendebat perdita mente.
a misera, assiduis quam luctibus externauit
spinosas Erycina serens in pectore curas,
illa tempestate, ferox quo ex tempore Theseus
egressus curuis e litoribus Piraei
attigit iniusti regis Cortinia tecta.
nam perhibent olim crudeli peste coactam
Androgeoneae poenas exsoluere caedis
electos iuuenes simul et decus innuptarum
Cecropiam solitam esse dapem dare Minotauro.
quis angusta malis cum moenia uexarentur,
ipse suum Theseus pro caris corpus Athenis
proicere· optauit potius quam talia Cretam
funera Cecropiae nec funera portarentur.
atque ita naue leui nitens ac lenibus auris
magnanimum ad Minoa uenit sedesque superbas.
hunc simul ac cupido conspexit lumine uirgo
regia, quam suauis exspirans castus odores
lectulus in molli complexu matris alebat,
quales Eurotae progignunt flumina myrtus,
auraue distinctos educit uerna colores,
non prius ex illo flagrantia declinauit
lumina, quam cuncto concepit corpore flammam
funditus atque imis exarsit tota medullis.
heu misere exagitans immiti corde furores
sancte puer, curis hominum qui gaudia misces,
quaeque regis Golgos ˙quaeque Idalium frondosum,
qualibus incensam iactastis mente puellam

[296]

fluctibus, in flauo saepe hòspite suspirantem!
quantos illa tulit languenti corde timores!
quanto saepe magis fulgore expalluit auri!
cum saeuum cupiens contra contendere monstrum
aut mortem appeteret Theseus aut praemia laudis.
non ingrata tamen frustra munuscula diuis
promittens tacito succendit uota labello.
nam uelut in summo quatientem brachia Tauro
quercum, aut conigeràm sudanti cortice pinum,
indomitus turbo contorquens flamine robur,
eruit (illa procul radicitus exturbata
prona cadit, late quaeuiscumque obuia frangens),
sic domito saeuum prostrauit corpore Theseus
nequiquam uanis iactantem cornua uentis.
inde pedem sospes multa cum laude reflexit
errabunda regens tenui uestigia filo,
ne labyrintheis e flexibus egredientem
tecti frustraretur inobseruabilis error.
sed quid ego a primo digressus carmine plura
commemorem, ut linquens genitoris filia uultum,
ut consanguineae complexum, ut denique matris,
quae misera in nata deperdita lamentata est,
omnibus his Thesei dulcem praeoptarit amorem
aut ut uecta ratis spumosa ad litora Diae,
aut ut eam deuincta   lumina somno
liquerit immemori discedens pectore coniunx?
saepe illam perhibent ardenti corde furentem
clarisonas imo fudisse e pectore uoces,
ac tum praeruptos tristem conscendere montes,
unde aciem in pelagi uastos protenderet aestus,
tum tremuli salis aduersas procurrere in undas
mollia nudatae tollentem tegmina surae,

[297]

atque haec extremis maestam dixisse querellis,
frigidulos udo singultus ore cientem.
'sicine me patriis auectam, perfide, ab aris,
perfide, deserto liquisti in litore, Theseu?
sicine discedens neglecto numine diuum,
immemor a deuota domum periuria portas?
nullane res potuit crudelis flectere mentis
consilium? tibi nulla fuit clementia praesto,
immite ut nostri uellet miserescere pectus?
at non haec quondam nobis promissa dedisti
uoce: mihi non haec miserae sperare iubebas,
sed conubia laeta, sed optatos hymenaeos,
quae cuncta aerei discerpunt irrita uenti.
tum iam nulla uiro iuranti femina credat,
nulla uiri speret sermones esse fideles;
quis dum aliquid cupiens animus praegestit apisci,
nil metuunt iurare, nihil promittere parcunt:
sed simul ac cupidae mentis satiata libido est,
dicta nihil metuere, nihil periuria curant.
certe ego te in medio uersantem turbine leti
eripui, et potius germanum amittere creui,
quam tibi fallaci supremo in tempore dessem.
pro quo dilaceranda feris dabor alitibusque
praeda, neque iniacta tumulabor mortua terra.
quaenam te genuit sola sub rupe leaena,
quod mare conceptum spumantibus exspuit undis,
quae Syrtis, quae Scylla rapax, quae uasta Carybdis,
talia qui reddis pro dulci praemia uita?
si tibi non cordi fuerant conubia nostra,
saeua quod horrebas prisci praecepta parentis,
at tamen in uestras potuisti ducere sedes,
quae tibi iucundo famularer serua labore,

candida permulcens liquidis uestigia lymphis,
purpureaue tuum consternens ueste cubile.
sed quid ego ignaris nequiquam conquerar aureis,
externata malo, quae nullis sensibus auctae
nec missas audire queunt nec reddere uoces?
ille autem prope iam mediis uersatur in undis,
nec quisquam apparet uacua mortalis in alga.
sic nimis insultans extremo tempore saeua
fors etiam nostris inuidit questibus auris.
Iuppiter omnipotens, utinam ne tempore primo
Gnosia Cecropiae tetigissent litora puppes,
indomito nec dira ferens stipendia tauro,
perfidus in Creta religasset nauita funem,
nec malus hic celans dulci crudelia forma
consilia, in nostris requiesset sedibus hospes!
nam quo me referam? quali spe perdita nitor?
Idomeneosne petam montes? a gurgite lato
discernens ponti truculentum diuidit aequor.
an patris auxilium sperem? quemne ipsa reliqui
respersum iuuenem fraterna caede secuta?
coniugis an fido consoler memet amore?
quine fugit lentos incuruans gurgite remos?
praeterea nullo litus, sola insula, tecto,
nec patet egressus pelagi cingentibus undis:
nulla fugae ratio, nulla spes: omnia muta,
omnia sunt deserta, ostentant omnia letum.
non tamen ante mihi languescent lumina morte,
nec prius a fesso secedent corpore sensus,
quam iustam a diuis exposcam prodita multam,
caelestumque fidem postrema comprecer hora.
quare facta uirum multantes uindice poena,
Eumenides, quibus anguino redimita capillo

frons exspirantis praeportat pectoris iras,
huc huc aduentate, meas audite querellas,
quas ego, uae miserae, extremis proferre medullis
cogor inops, ardens, amenti caeca furore.
quae quoniam uerae nascuntur pectore ab imo,
uos nolite pati nostrum uanescere luctum,
sed quali solam Theseus me mente reliquit,
tali mente, deae, funestet seque suosque.'
has postquam maesto profudit pectore uoces,
supplicium saeuis exposcens anxia factis,
annuit inuicto caelestum numine rector.
quo motu tellus atque horrida contremuerunt
aequora concussitque micantia sidera mundus.
ipse autem caeca mentem caligine Theseus
consitus oblito dimisit pectore cuncta,
quae mandata prius constanti mente tenebat,
dulcia nec maesto sustollens signa parenti
sospitem Erechtheum se ostendit uisere portum.
namque ferunt olim, classi cum moenia diuae
linquentem natum uentis concrederet Aegeus,
talia complexum iuueni mandata dedisse.
' nate mihi longa iucundior unice uita,
nate, ego quem in dubios cogor dimittere casus,
reddite in extrema nuper mihi fine senectae,
quandoquidem fortuna mea ac tua feruida uirtus
eripit inuito mihi te, cui languida nondum
lumina sunt nati cara saturata figura,
non ego te gaudens laetanti pectore mittam,
nec te ferre sinam fortunae signa secundae,
sed primum multas expromam mente querellas,
canitiem terra atque infuso puluere foedans,
inde infecta uago suspendam lintea malo,
nostros ut luctus nostraeque incendia mentis

carbasus obscurata dicet ferrugine Hibera.
quod tibi si sancti concesserit incola Itoni,
quae nostrum genus, has sedes defendere Erechthi
annuit, ut tauri respergas sanguine dextram,
tum uero facito ut memori tibi condita corde
haec uigeant mandata, nec ulla oblitteret aetas;
ut simul ac nostros inuisent lumina collis,
funestam antennae deponant undique uestem,
candidaque intorti sustollant uela rudentes,
quam primum cernens ut laeta gaudia mente
agnoscam, cum te reducem aetas prospera sistet.'
haec mandata prius constanti mente tenentem
Thesea ceu pulsae uentorum flamine nubes
aereum niuei montis liquere cacumen.
at pater, ut summa prospectum ex arce petebat,
anxia in assiduos absumens lumina fletus,
cum primum inflati conspexit lintea ueli,
praecipitem sese scopulorum e uertice iecit,
amissum credens immiti Thesea fato.
sic funesta domus ingressus tecta paterna
morte ferox Theseus, qualem Minoidi luctum
obtulerat mente immemori talem ipse recepit.
quae tamen aspectans cedentem maesta carinam
multiplices animo uoluebat saucia curas.
at parte ex alia florens uolitabat Iacchus
cum thiaso Satyrorum et Nysigenis Silenis,
te quaerens, Ariadna, tuoque incensus amore.
qui tum alacres passim lymphata mente furebant
euhoe bacchantes, euhoe capita inflectentes.
harum pars tecta quatiebant cuspide thyrsos,
pars e diuulso iactabant membra iuuenco,

pars sese tortis serpentibus incingebant,
pars obscura cauis celebrabant orgia cistis,
orgia, quae frustra cupiunt audire profani,
plangebant aliae proceris tympana palmis,
aut tereti tenuis tinnitus aere ciebant,
multis raucisonos efflabant cornua bombos
barbaraque horribili stridebat tibia cantu.
talibus amplifice uestis decorata figuris
puluinar complexa suo uelabat amictu.
quae postquam cupide spectando Thessala pubes
expleta est, sanctis coepit decedere diuis.
hic, qualis flatu placidum mare matutino
horrificans Zephyrus procliuas incitat undas,
aurora exoriente uagi sub limina Solis :
quae tarde primum clementi flamine pulsae
procedunt, leni et resonant plangore cachinni,
post uento crescente magis magis increbescunt,
purpureaque procul nantes ab luce refulgent :
sic tum uestibuli linquentis regia tecta
ad se quisque uago passim pede discedebant.
quorum post abitum princeps e uertice Pelei
aduenit Chiron portans siluestria dona :
nam quodcumque ferunt campi, quos Thessala magnis
montibus ora creat, quos propter fluminis undas
aura parit flores tepidi fecunda Fauoni,
hos indistinctis plexos tulit ipse corollis,
quo permulsa domus iucundo risit odore.
confestim Penios adest, uiridantia Tempe,
Tempe, quae siluae cingunt super impendentes,
†Minosim† linquens †doris† celebranda choreis,
non uacuos : namque ille tulit radicitus altas
fagos ac recto proceras stipite laurus,
non sine nutanti platano lentaque sorore

flammati Phaethontis et aerea cupressu.
haec circum sedes late contexta locauit,
uestibulum ut molli uelatum fronde uireret.
post hunc consequitur sollerti corde Prometheus,
extenuata gerens ueteris uestigia poenae,
quam quondam silici restrictus membra catena
persoluit pendens e uerticibus praeruptis.
inde pater diuum sancta cum coniuge natisque
aduenit caelo, te solum, Phoebe, relinquens,
unigenamque simul cultricem montibus Iri :
Pelea nam tecum pariter soror aspernata est,
nec Thetidis taedas uoluit celebrare iugalis.
qui postquam niueis flexerunt sedibus artus,
large multiplici constructae sunt dape mensae,
cum interea infirmo quatientes corpora motu
ueridicos Parcae coeperunt edere cantus.
his corpus tremulum complectens undique uestis
candida purpurea talos incinxerat ora,
at roseo niueae residebant uertice uittae,
aeternumque manus carpebant rite laborem.
laeua colum molli lana retinebat amictum,
dextera tum leuiter deducens fila supinis
formabat digitis, tum prono in pollice torquens
libratum tereti uersabat turbine fusum,
atque ita decerpens aequabat semper opus dens,
laneaque aridulis haerebant morsa labellis,
quae prius in leui fuerant exstantia filo :
ante pedes autem candentis mollia lanae
uellera uirgati custodibant calathisci.
haec tum clarisona pellentes uellera uoce
talia diuino fuderunt carmine fata,

carmine, perfidiae quod post nulla arguet aetas.
O decus eximium magnis uirtutibus augens,
Emathiae tutamen opis, clarissime nato,
accipe, quod laeta tibi pandunt luce sorores,
ueridicum oraclum : sed uos, quae fata secuntur,
currite ducentes subtegmina, currite, fusi.
adueniet tibi iam portans optata maritis
Hesperus, adueniet fausto cum sidere coniunx,
quae tibi flexanimo mentis perfundat amorem,
languidulosque paret tecum coniungere somnos,
leuia substernens robusto brachia collo.
currite ducentes subtegmina, currite, fusi.
nulla domus tales umquam contexit amores,
nullus amor tali coniunxit foedere amantes,
qualis adest Thetidi, qualis concordia Peleo.
currite ducentes subtegmina, currite, fusi.
nascetur uobis expers terroris Achilles,
hostibus haud tergo, sed forti pectore notus,
qui persaepe uago uictor certamine cursus'
flammea praeuertet celeris uestigia ceruae.
currite ducentes subtegmina, currite, fusi.
non illi quisquam bello se conferet heros,
cum Phrygii Teucro manabunt sanguine campi,
Troicaque obsidens longinquo moenia bello,
periuri Pelopis uastabit tertius heres.
currite ducentes subtegmina, currite, fusi.
illius egregias uirtutes claraque facta
saepe fatebuntur natorum in funere matres,
cum incuruo canos soluent a uertice crines,
putridaque infirmis uariabunt pectora palmis.
currite ducentes subtegmina, currite, fusi.
namque uelut densas praecerpens cultor aristas

sole sub ardenti flauentia demetit arua,

. . . .

Troiugenum infesto prosternens corpora ferro.
currite ducentes subtegmina, currite, fusi.
testis erit magnis uirtutibus unda Scamandri,
quae passim rapido diffunditur Hellesponto,
cuius iter caesis angustans corporum aceruis
alta tepefaciet permixta flumina caede.
currite ducentes subtegmina, currite, fusi.
denique testis erit morti quoque reddita praeda,
cum teres excelso coaceruatum aggere bustum
excipiet niueos perculsae uirginis artus.
currite ducentes subtegmina, currite, fusi.
nam simul ac fessis dederit fors copiam Achiuis
urbis Dardaniae Neptunia soluere uincla,
alta Polyxenia madefient caede sepulcra :
quae, uelut ancipiti succumbens uictima ferro,
proiciet truncum summisso poplite corpus.
currite ducentes subtegmina, currite, fusi.
quare agite optatos animi coniungite amores.
accipiat coniunx felici foedere diuam,
dedatur cupido iam dudum nupta marito.
currite ducentes subtegmina, currite, fusi.
non illam nutrix orienti luce reuisens
hesterno collum poterit circumdare filo,
currite ducentes subtegmina, currite, fusi.
anxia nec mater discordis maesta puellae
secubitu caros mittet sperare nepotes.
currite ducentes subtegmina, currite, fusi.
talia praefantes quondam felicia Pelei
carmina diuino cecinerunt pectore Parcae.
praesentes namque ante domos inuisere castas
heroum, et sese mortali ostendere coetu,

[305]

caelicolae nondum spreta pietate solebant.
saepe pater diuum templo in fulgente reuisens,
annua cum festis uenissent sacra diebus,
conspexit terra centum procumbere tauros.
saepe uagus Liber Parnasi uertice summo
Thyadas effusis euantis crinibus egit,
cum Delphi tota certatim ex urbe ruentes
acciperent laeti diuum fumantibus aris.
saepe in letifero belli certamine Mauors
aut rapidi Tritonis hera aut Ramnusia uirgo
armatas hominum est praesens hortata cateruas.
sed postquam tellus scelere est imbuta nefando,
iustitiamque omnes cupida de mente fugarunt,
perfudere manus fraterno sanguine fratres,
destitit extinctos natus lugere parentes,
optauit genitor primaeui funera nati,
liber ut innuptae poteretur flore nouercae,
ignaro mater substernens se impia nato
impia non uerita est diuos scelerare parentes,
omnia fanda nefanda malo permixta furore
iustificam nobis mentem auertere deorum.
quare nec talis dignantur uisere coetus,
nec se contingi patiuntur lumine claro.

Etsi me assiduo confectum cura dolore
    seuocat a doctis, Ortale, uirginibus,
nec potis est dulcis Musarum expromere fetus
    mens animi, tantis fluctuat ipsa malis:
namque mei nuper Lethaeo in gurgite fratris
    pallidulum manans alluit unda pedem,
Troia Rhoeteo quem subter litore tellus
    ereptum nostris obterit ex oculis.
alloquar, audiero numquam   loquentem,

numquam ego te, uita frater amabilior,
    aspiciam posthac? at certe semper amabo,
    semper maesta tua carmina morte tegam,
qualia sub densis ramorum concinit umbris
    Daulias, absumptei fata gemens Itylei.
sed tamen in tantis maeroribus, Ortale, mitto
    haec expressa tibi carmina Battiadae,
ne tua dicta uagis nequiquam credita uentis
    effluxisse meo forte putes animo.
ut missum sponsi furtiuo munere malum
    procurrit casto uirginis e gremio,
quod miserae oblitae molli sub ueste locatum,
    dum aduentu matris prosilit, excutitur :
atque illud prono praeceps agitur decursu,
    huic manat tristi conscius ore rubor.

LXVI

OMNIA qui magni dispexit lumina mundi,
    qui stellarum ortus comperit atque obitus,
flammeus ut rapidi solis nitor obscuretur,
    ut cedant certis sidera temporibus,
ut Triuiam furtim sub Latmia saxa relegans
    dulcis amor giro deuocet aereo :
idem me ille Conon caelesti numine uidit
    e Beroniceo uertice caesariem
fulgentem clare, quam multis illa dearum
    leuia protendens brachia pollicita est,
qua rex tempestate nouo auctus hymenaeo
    uastatum finis iuerat Assyrios,
dulcia nocturnae portans uestigia rixae,
    quam de uirgineis gesserat exuuiis.
estne nouis nuptis odio Venus? idque parentum

frustratur falsis gaudia lacrimulis,
ubertim thalami quas intra limina fundunt?
non, ita me diui, uera gemunt, iuerint.
id mea me multis docuit regina querellis
inuisente nouo proelia torua uiro.
et tu non orbum luxti deserta cubile,
sed fratris cari flebile discidium?
cum penitus maestas exedit cura medullas!
ut tibi tunc toto pectore sollicitae
sensibus ereptis mens excidit! at te ego certe
cognoram a parua uirgine magnanimam.
anne bonum oblita es facinus, quo regium adepta es
coniugium, quod non fortior ausit alis?
sed tum maesta uirum mittens quae uerba locuta es!
Iuppiter, ut tristi lumina saepe manu!
quis te mutauit tantus deus? an quod amantes
non longe a caro corpore abesse uolunt?
atque ibi me cunctis pro dulci coniuge diuis
non sine taurino sanguine pollicita es,
si reditum tetulisset. is haut in tempore longo
captam Asiam Aegypti finibus addiderat.
quis ego pro factis caelesti reddita coetu
pristina uota nouo munere dissoluo.
inuita, o regina, tuo de uertice cessi,
inuita: adiuro teque tuumque caput,
digna ferat quod siquis inaniter adiurarit:
sed qui se ferro postulet esse parem?
ille quoque euersus mons est, quem maximum in oris
progenies Thiae clara superuehitur,
cum Medi peperere nouum mare, cumque iuuentus
per medium classi barbara nauit Athon.
quid facient crines, cum ferro talia cedant?

Iuppiter, ut Chalybon omne genus pereat,
et qui principio sub terra quaerere uenas
  institit ac ferri stringere duritiem!
abiunctae paulo ante comae mea fata sorores
  lugebant, cum se Memnonis Aethiopis
unigena impellens nutantibus aera pennis
  obtulit Arsinoes Locridos ales equos,
isque per aetherias me tollens abuolat umbras
  et Veneris casto collocat in gremio.
ipsa suum Zephyritis eo famulum legarat,
  Graia Canopieis incola litoribus.
hic iuueni Ismario ne solum in limine caeli
  ex Ariadneis aurea temporibus
fixa corona foret, sed nos quoque fulgeremus
  deuotae flaui uerticis exuuiae,
uuidulum a fluctu cedentem ad templa deum me
  sidus in antiquis diua nouum posuit.
Virginis et saeui contingens namque Leonis
  lumina, Callisto iuxta Lycaoniam,
uertor in occasum, tardum dux ante Booten,
  qui uix sero alto mergitur Oceano.
sed quamquam me nocte premunt uestigia diuum,
  lux autem canae Tethyi restituit,
(pace tua fari hic liceat, Ramnusia uirgo,
  namque ego non ullo uera timore tegam,
nec si me infestis discerpent sidera dictis,
  condita quin ueri pectoris euoluam):
non his tam laetor rebus, quam me afore semper,
  afore me a dominae uertice discrucior,
quicum ego, dum uirgo quondam fuit, omnibus expers
  unguentis, una milia multa bibi.
nunc uos, optato quas iunxit lumine taeda,

non post unanimis corpora coniugibus
tradite nudantes reiecta ueste papillas,
  quin iucunda mihi munera libet onyx,
  uester onyx, casto petitis quae iura cubili.
sed quae se impuro dedit adulterio,
illius a mala dona leuis bibat irrita puluis :
  namque ego ab indignis praemia nulla peto.
sed magis, o nuptae, semper concordia uestras
  semper amor sedes incolat assiduus.
tu uero, regina, tuens cum sidera diuam
  placabis festis luminibus Venerem,
sanguinis expertem non †uestris† esse tuum me,
  sed potius largis affice muneribus.
sidera corruerint utinam ! coma regia fiam,
  proximus Hydrochoi fulgeret Oarion !

LXVII

CATVLLVS

O DVLCI iucunda uiro, iucunda parenti,
  salue, teque bona Iuppiter auctet ope,
ianua, quam Balbo dicunt seruisse benigne
  olim, cum sedes ipse senex tenuit,
quamque ferunt rursus uoto seruisse maligno,
  postquam es porrecto facta marita sene.
dic age dum nobis, quare mutata feraris
  in dominum ueterem deseruisse fidem.

IANVA

Non (ita Caecilio placeam, cui tradita nunc sum)
  culpa mea est, quamquam dicitur esse mea,
nec peccatum a me quisquam pote dicere quicquam :
  †uerum istius populi ianua qui te facit†,

qui, quacumque aliquid reperitur non bene factum,
  ad me omnes clamant: ianua, culpa tua est.

CATVLLVS

Non istuc satis est uno te dicere uerbo,
  sed facere ut quiuis sentiat et uideat.

IANVA

Qui possum? nemo quaerit nec scire laborat.

CATVLLVS

Nos uolumus: nobis dicere ne dubita.

IANVA

Primum igitur, uirgo quod fertur tradita nobis,
  falsum est. non illam uir prior attigerit,
languidior tenera cui pendens sicula beta
  numquam se mediam sustulit ad tunicam:
sed pater illius nati uiolasse cubile
  dicitur et miseram conscelerasse domum,
siue quod impia mens caeco flagrabat amore,
  seu quod iners sterili semine natus erat,
ut quaerendum unde unde foret neruosius illud,
  quod posset zonam soluere uirgineam.

CATVLLVS

Egregium narras mira pietate parentem,
  qui ipse sui nati minxerit in gremium.

IANVA

Atqui non solum hoc se dicit cognitum habere
  Brixia Chinea supposita specula,
flauus quam molli percurrit flumine Mella,
  Brixia Veronae mater amata meae,
sed de Postumio et Corneli narrat amore,
  cum quibus illa malum fecit adulterium.
dixerit hic aliquis: quid? tu istaec, ianua, nosti?
  cui numquam domini limine abesse licet,
nec populum auscultare, sed hic suffixa tigillo

[311]

tantum operire soles aut aperire domum?
saepe illam audiui furtiua uoce loquentem
  solam cum ancillis haec sua flagitia,
nomine dicentem quos diximus, ut pote quae mi
  speraret nec linguam esse nec auriculam.
praeterea addebat quendam, quem dicere nolo
  nomine, ne tollat rubra supercilia.
longus homo est, magnas cui lites intulit olim
  falsum mendaci uentre puerperium.

LXVIII

Qvod mihi fortuna casuque oppressus acerbo
  conscriptum hoc lacrimis mittis epistolium,
naufragum ut eiectum spumantibus aequoris undis
  subleuem et a mortis limine restituam,
quem neque sancta Venus molli requiescere somno
  desertum in lecto caelibe perpetitur,
nec ueterum dulci scriptorum carmine Musae
  oblectant, cum mens anxia peruigilat:
id gratum est mihi, me quoniam tibi dicis amicum,
  muneraque et Musarum hinc petis et Veneris:
sed tibi ne mea sint ignota incommoda, Malli,
  neu me odisse putes hospitis officium,
accipe, quis merser fortunae fluctibus ipse,
  ne amplius a misero dona beata petas.
tempore quo primum uestis mihi tradita pura est,
  iucundum cum aetas florida uer ageret,
multa satis lusi: non est dea nescia nostri,
  quae dulcem curis miscet amaritiem:
sed totum hoc studium luctu fraterna mihi mors
  abstulit. o misero frater adempte mihi,
tu mea tu moriens fregisti commoda, frater,

tecum una tota est nostra sepulta domus,
omnia tecum una perierunt gaudia nostra,
  quae tuus in uita dulcis alebat amor.
cuius ego interitu tota de mente fugaui
  haec studia atque omnis delicias animi.
quare, quod scribis Veronae turpe Catullo
  esse, quod hic quisquis de meliore nota
frigida deserto tepefacsit membra cubili,
  id, Malli, non est turpe, magis miserum est.
ignosces igitur, si, quae mihi luctus ademit,
  haec tibi non tribuo munera, cum nequeo.
nam, quod scriptorum non magna est copia apud me,
  hoc fit, quod Romae uiuimus : illa domus,
illa mihi sedes, illic mea carpitur aetas :
  huc una ex multis capsula me sequitur.
quod cum ita sit, nolim statuas nos mente maligna
  id facere aut animo non satis ingenuo,
quod tibi non utriusque petenti copia posta est :
  ultro ego deferrem, copia siqua foret.

*

Non possum reticere, deae, qua me Allius in re
  iuuerit aut quantis iuuerit officiis,
ne fugiens saeclis obliuiscentibus aetas
  illius hoc caeca nocte tegat studium :
sed dicam uobis, uos porro dicite multis
  milibus et facite haec carta loquatur anus.

. . . .

  notescatque magis mortuus atque magis,
nec tenuem texens sublimis aranea telam
  in deserto Alli nomine opus faciat.
nam, mihi quam dederit duplex Amathusia curam,
  scitis, et in quo me corruerit genere,
cum tantum arderem quantum Trinacria rupes

lymphaque in Oetaeis Malia Thermopylis,
maesta neque assiduo tabescere pupula fletu
cessaret tristique imbre madere genae.
qualis in aerei perlucens uertice montis
riuus muscoso prosilit e lapide,
qui cum de prona praeceps est ualle uolutus,
per medium densi transit iter populi,
dulce uiatori lasso in sudore leuamen,
cum grauis exustos aestus hiulcat agros:
hic, uelut in nigro iactatis turbine nautis
lenius aspirans aura secunda uenit
iam prece Pollucis, iam Castoris implorata,
tale fuit nobis Allius auxilium.
is clausum lato patefecit limite campum,
isque domum nobis isque dedit dominam,
ad quam communes exerceremus amores.
quo mea se molli candida diua pede
intulit et trito fulgentem in limine plantam
innixsa arguta constituit solea.
coniugis ut quondam flagrans aduenit amore
Protesilaeam Laudamia domum
inceptam frustra, nondum cum sanguine sacro
hostia caelestis pacificasset heros.
nil mihi tam ualde placeat, Ramnusia uirgo,
quod temere inuitis suscipiatur heris.
quam ieiuna pium desideret ara cruorem,
docta est amisso Laudamia uiro,
coniugis ante coacta noui dimittere collum,
quam ueniens una atque altera rursus hiems
noctibus in longis auidum saturasset amorem,
posset ut abrupto uiuere coniugio,
quod scibant Parcae non longo tempore abisse,

si miles muros isset ad Iliacos.
nam tum Helenae raptu primores Argiuorum
    coeperat ad sese Troia ciere uiros,
Troia (nefas) commune sepulcrum Asiae Europaeque,
    Troia uirum et uirtutum omnium acerba cinis,
qualiter et nostro letum miserabile fratri
    attulit. ei misero frater adempte mihi,
ei misero fratri iucundum lumen ademptum,
    tecum una tota est nostra sepulta domus,
omnia tecum una perierunt gaudia nostra,
    quae tuus in uita dulcis alebat amor.
quem nunc tam longe non inter nota sepulcra
    nec prope cognatos compositum cineris,
sed Troia obscena, Troia infelice sepultum
    detinet extremo terra aliena solo.
ad quam tum properans fertur simul undique pubes
    Graeca penetralis deseruisse focos,
ne Paris abducta gauisus libera moecha
    otia pacato degeret in thalamo.
quo tibi tum casu, pulcerrima Laudamia,
    ereptum est uita dulcius atque anima
coniugium : tanto te absorbens uertice amoris
    aestus in abruptum detulerat barathrum,
quale ferunt Grai Pheneum prope Cylleneum
    siccare emulsa pingue palude solum,
quod quondam caesis montis fodisse medullis
    audit falsiparens Amphitryoniades,
tempore quo certa Stymphalia monstra sagitta
    perculit imperio deterioris heri,
pluribus ut caeli tereretur ianua diuis,
    Hebe nec longa uirginitate foret.
sed tuus altus amor barathro fuit altior illo,

qui actutum domitum ferre iugum docuit.
nam neque tam carum confecto aetate parenti
   una caput seri nata nepotis alit,
qui cum diuitiis uix tandem inuentus auitis
   nomen testatas intulit in tabulas,
impia derisi gentilis gaudia tollens,
   suscitat a cano uolturium capiti :
nec tantum ṇiueo gauisa est ulla columbo
   compar, quae multo dicitur improbius
oscula mordenti semper decerpere rostro,
   quam cum praecipue multiuola est mulier.
sed tu horum magnos uicisti sola furores,
   ut semel es flauo conciliata uiro.
aut nihil aut paulo cui tum concedere digna
   lux mea se nostrum contulit in gremium,
quam circumcursans hinc illinc saepe Cupido
   fulgebat crocina candidus in tunica.
quae tamen etsi uno non est contenta Catullo,
   rara uerecundae furta feremus herae,
ne nimium simus stultorum more molesti.
   saepe etiam Iuno, maxima caelicolum,
coniugis in culpa flagrantem contudit iram,
   noscens omniuoli plurima facta Iouis.
at, quia nec diuis homines componier aequum est,

  . . . .
. . . .

   ingratum tremuli tolle parentis onus.
nec tamen illa mihi dexstra deducta paterna
   fraglantem Assyrio uenit odore domum,
sed furtiua dedit mira munuscula nocte,
   ipsius ex ipso dempta uiri gremio.
quare illud satis est, si nobis is datur unis

[316]

quem lapide illa diem candidiore notat.
hoc tibi, quod potui, confectum carmine munus
    pro multis, Alli, redditur officiis,
ne uestrum scabra tangat rubigine nomen
    haec atque illa dies atque alia atque alia.
huc addent diui quam plurima, quae Themis olim
    antiquis solita est munera ferre piis.
seitis felices et tu simul et tua uita,
    et domus in qua olim lusimus et domina,
et qui principio nobis †terram dedit aufert†,
    a quo sunt primo omnia nata bona,
et longe ante omnes mihi quae me carior ipso est,
    lux mea, qua uiua uiuere dulce mihi est.

LXIX

Noli admirari, quare tibi femina nulla,
    Rufe, uelit tenerum supposuisse femur,
non si illam rarae labefactes munere uestis
    aut perluciduli deliciis lapidis.
laedit te quaedam mala fabula, qua tibi fertur
    ualle sub alarum trux habitare caper.
hunc metuunt omnes : neque mirum : nam mala ualde est
    bestia, nec quicum bella puella cubet.
quare aut crudelem nasorum interfice pestem,
    aut admirari desine cur fugiunt.

LXX

Nvlli se dicit mulier mea nubere málle
    quam mihi, non si se Iuppiter ipse petat.
dicit : sed mulier cupido quod dicit amanti,
    in uento et rapida scribere oportet aqua.

LXXI

Sɪ quoi, Virro, bono sacer introsum obstitit hircus,
    aut si quam merito tarda podagra secat,
aemulus iste tuus, qui uestrum exercet amorem,
    mirifice est a te nactus utrumque malum.
nam quotiens futuit, totiens ulciscitur ambos :
    illam affligit odore, ipse perit podagra.

LXXII

Dɪcᴇʙᴀs quondam solum te nosse Catullum,
    Lesbia, nec prae me uelle tenere Iouem.
dilexi tum te non tantum ut uulgus amicam,
    sed pater ut natos diligit et generos.
nunc te cognoui : quare etsi impensius uror,
    multo mei tamen es uilior et leuior.
qui potis est? inquis. Quod amantem iniuria talis
    cogit amare magis, sed bene uelle minus.

LXXIII

Dᴇsɪɴᴇ de quoquam quisquam bene uelle mereri,
    aut aliquem fieri posse putare pium.
omnia sunt ingrata, nihil fecisse benigne
    prodest, immo etiam taedet obestque magis ;
ut mihi, quem nemo grauius nec acerbius urget,
    quam modo qui me unum atque unicum amicum habuit.

LXXIV

Gᴇʟʟɪᴠs audierat patruum obiurgare solere,
    siquis delicias diceret aut faceret.
hoc ne ipsi accideret, patrui perdepsuit ipsam
    uxorem et patruum reddidit Harpocratem.
quod uoluit fecit : nam, quamuis irrumet ipsum
    nunc patruum, uerbum non faciet patruus.

[318]

LXXV

Hvc est mens deducta tua, mea Lesbia, culpa,
  atque ita se officio perdidit ipsa suo,
ut iam nec bene uelle queat tibi, si optima fias,
  nec desistere amare, omnia si facias.

LXXVI

SIQVA recordanti benefacta priora uoluptas
  est homini, cum se cogitat esse pium,
nec sanctam uiolasse fidem, nec foedere in ullo
  diuum ad fallendos numine abusum homines,
multa parata manent in longa aetate, Catulle,
  ex hoc ingrato gaudia amore tibi.
nam quaecumque homines bene cuiquam aut dicere possunt
  aut facere, haec a te dictaque factaque sunt.
omnia quae ingratae perierunt credita menti.
  quare iam te cur amplius excrucies?
quin tu animo offirmas atque istinc te ipse reducis,
  et dis inuitis desinis esse miser?
difficile est longum subito deponere amorem.
  difficile est, uerum hoc qua lubet efficias:
una salus haec est, hoc est tibi peruincendum,
  hoc facias, siue id non pote siue pote.
o di, si uestrum est misereri, aut si quibus umquam
  extremam iam ipsa in morte tulistis opem,
me miserum aspicite et, si uitam puriter egi,
  eripite hanc pestem perniciemque mihi,
sei mihi surrepens imos ut torpor in artus
  expulit ex omni pectore laetitias.
non iam illud quaero, contra ut me diligat illa,
  aut, quod non potis est, esse pudica uelit:

ipse ualere opto et taetrum hunc deponere morbum.
o di, reddite mi hoc pro pietate mea.

LXXVII

RVFE mihi frustra ac nequiquam credite amice
  (frustra? immo magno cum pretio atque malo),
sicine subrepsti mei, atque intestina perurens
  ei misero eripuisti omnia nostra bona?
eripuisti, heu heu nostrae crudele uenenum
  uitae, heu heu nostrae pestis amicitiae.
sed nunc id doleo, quod purae pura puellae
  suauia comminxit spurca saliua tua.
uerum id non impune feres: nam te omnia saecla
  noscent, et qui sis fama loquetur anus.

LXXVIII

GALLVS habet fratres, quorum est lepidissima coniunx
  alterius, lepidus filius alterius.
Gallus homo est bellus: nam dulces iungit amores,
  cum puero ut bello bella puella cubet.
Gallus homo est stultus, nec se uidet esse maritum,
  qui patruus patrui monstret adulterium.

LXXIX

LESBIVS est pulcer. quid ni? quem Lesbia malit
  quam te cum tota gente, Catulle, tua.
sed tamen hic pulcer uendat cum gente Catullum,
  si tria natorum suauia reppererit.

LXXX

QVID dicam, Gelli, quare rosea ista labella
  hiberna fiant candidiora niue,
mane domo cum exis et cum te octaua quiete

e molli longo suscitat hora die?
nescio quid certe est: an uere fama susurrat
grandia te medii tenta uorare uiri?
sic certe est: clamant Victoris rupta miselli
ilia, et emulso labrá notata sero.

LXXXI

NEMONE in tanto potuit populo esse, Iuuenti,
  bellus homo, quem tu diligere inciperes,
praeterquam iste tuus moribunda ab sede Pisauri
  hospes inaurata pallidior statua,
qui tibi nunc cordi est, quem tu praeponere nobis
  audes, et nescis quod facinus facias?

LXXXII

QVINTI, si tibi uis oculos debere Catullum
  aut aliud si quid carius est oculis,
eripere ei noli, multo quod carius illi
  est oculis seu quid carius est oculis.

LXXXIII

LESBIA mi praesente uiro mala plurima dicit:
  haec illi fatuo maxima laetitia est.
mule, nihil sentis: si nostri oblita taceret,
  sana esset: nunc quod gannit et obloquitur,
non solum meminit, sed, quae multo acrior est res,
  irata est: hoc est, uritur et loquitur.

LXXXIV

CHOMMODA dicebat, si quando commoda uellet
  dicere, et insidias Arrius hinsidias,
et tum mirifice sperabat se esse locutum,

cum quantum poterat dixerat hinsidias.
credo, sic mater, sic Liber auunculus eius,
    sic maternus auus dixerat atque auia.
hoc misso in Syriam requierant omnibus aures :
    audibant eadem haec leniter et leuiter,
nec sibi postilla metuebant talia uerba,
    cum subito affertur nuntius horribilis,
Ionios fluctus, postquam illuc Arrius isset,
    iam non Ionios esse, sed Hionios.

LXXXV

ODI et amo : quare id faciam, fortasse requiris.
    nescio, sed fieri sentio et excrucior.

LXXXVI

QVINTIA formosa est multis, mihi candida, longa,
    recta est : haec ego sic singula confiteor.
totum illud formosa nego : nam nulla uenustas,
    nulla in tam magno est corpore mica salis.
Lesbia formosa est, quae cum pulcerrima tota est,
    tum omnibus una omnis surripuit Veneres.

LXXXVII

NVLLA potest mulier tantum se dicere amatam
    uere, quantum a me Lesbia amata mea es.
nulla fides nullo fuit umquam in foedere tanta,
    quanta in amore tuo ex parte reperta mea est.

LXXXVIII

QVID facit is, Gelli, qui cum matre atque sorore
    prurit et abiectis peruigilat tunicis ?

quid facit is, patruum qui non sinit esse maritum?
ecquid scis quantum suscipiat sceleris?
suscipit, o Gelli, quantum non ultima Tethys
   nec genitor Nympharum abluit Oceanus:
nam nihil est quicquam sceleris, quo prodeat ultra,
   non si demisso se ipse uoret capite.

LXXXIX

GELLIVS est tenuis: quid ni? cui tam bona mater
   tamque ualens uiuat tamque uenusta soror
tamque bonus patruus tamque omnia plena puellis
   cognatis, quare is desinat esse macer?
qui ut nihil attingat, nisi quod fas tangere non est,
   quantumuis quare sit macer inuenies.

XC

NASCATVR Magus ex Gelli matrisque nefando
   coniugio et discat Persicum aruspicium:
nam magus ex matre et nato gignatur oportet,
   si uera est Persarum impia religio,
natus ut accepto ueneretur carmine diuos
   omentum in flamma pingue liquefaciens.

XCI

NON ideo, Gelli, sperabam te mihi fidum
   in misero hoc nostro, hoc perdito amore fore,
quod te cognossem bene constantemue putarem
   aut posse a turpi mentem inhibere probro;
sed neque quod matrem nec germanam esse uidebam
   hanc tibi, cuius me magnus edebat amor.
et quamuis tecum multo coniungerer usu,
   non satis id causae credideram esse tibi.
tu satis id duxti: tantum tibi gaudium in omni
   culpa est, in quacumque est aliquid sceleris.

[323]

XCII

Lesbia mi dicit semper male nec tacet umquam
de me: Lesbia me dispeream nisi amat.
quo signo? quia sunt totidem mea: deprecor illam
assidue, uerum dispeream nisi amo.

XCIII

Nil nimium studeo, Caesar, tibi uelle placere,
nec scire utrum sis albus an ater homo.

XCIV

Mentvla moechatur. moechatur mentula certe.
hoc est quod dicunt, ipsa olera olla legit.

XCV

Zmyrna mei Cinnae nonam post denique messem
quam coepta est nonamque edita post hiemem,
milia cum interea quingenta Hortensius uno
. . . .
Zmyrna cauas Satrachi penitus mittetur ad undas,
Zmyrnam cana diu saecula peruoluent.
at Volusi annales Paduam morientur ad ipsam
et laxas scombris saepe dabunt tunicas.
parua mei mihi sint cordi monimenta . . .,
at populus tumido gaudeat Antimacho.

XCVI

Si quicquam mutis gratum acceptumue sepulcris
accidere a nostro, Calue, dolore potest,
quo desiderio ueteres renouamus amores
atque olim missas flemus amicitias,
certe non tanto mors immatura dolorei'st
Quintiliae, quantum gaudet amore tuo.

XCVII

Non (ita me di ament) quicquam referre putaui,
  utrumne os an culum olfacerem Aemilio.
nilo mundius hoc, niloque immundius illud,
  uerum etiam culus mundior et melior:
nam sine dentibus hic: dentis os sesquipedalis,
  gingiuas uero ploxeni habet ueteris,
praeterea rictum qualem diffissus in aestu
  meientis mulae cunnus habere solet.
hic futuit multas et se facit esse uenustum,
  et non pistrino traditur atque asino?
quem siqua attingit, non illam posse putemus
  aegroti culum lingere carnificis?

XCVIII

In te, si in quemquam, dici pote, putide Victi,
  id quod uerbosis dicitur et fatuis.
ista cum lingua, si usus ueniat tibi, possis
  culos et crepidas lingere carpatinas.
si nos omnino uis omnes perdere, Victi,
  hiscas: omnino quod cupis efficies.

XCIX

Svrripvi tibi, dum ludis, mellite Iuuenti,
  suauiolum dulci dulcius ambrosia.
uerum id non impune tuli: namque amplius horam
  suffixum in summa me memini esse cruce,
dum tibi me purgo nec possum fletibus ullis
  tantillum uestrae demere saeuitiae.
nam simul id factum est, multis diluta labella
  guttis abstersisti omnibus articulis,

ne quicquam nostro contractum ex ore maneret,
  tamquam commictae spurca saliua lupae.
praeterea infestum misero me tradere amori
  non cessasti omnique excruciare modo,
ut mi ex ambrosia mutatum iam foret illud
  suauiolum tristi tristius elleboro.
quam quoniam poenam misero proponis amori,
  numquam iam posthac basia surripiam.

C

Caelivs Aufilenum et Quintius Aufilenam
  flos Veronensum depereunt iuuenum,
hic fratrem, ille sororem. hoc est, quod dicitur, illud
  fraternum uere dulce sodalicium.
qui faueam potius? Caeli, tibi: nam tua nobis
  perfecta †exigitur† unica amicitia,
cum uesana meas torreret flamma medullas.
  sis felix, Caeli, sis in amore potens.

CI

Mvltas per gentes et multa per aequora uectus
  aduenio has miseras, frater, ad inferias,
ut te postremo donarem munere mortis
  et mutam nequiquam alloquerer cinerem.
quandoquidem fortuna mihi tete abstulit ipsum,
  heu miser indigne frater adempte mihi,
nunc tamen interea haec prisco quae more parentum
  tradita sunt tristi munere ad inferias,
accipe fraterno multum manantia fletu,
  atque in perpetuum, frater, aue atque uale.

CII

Sı quicquam tacito commissum est fido ab amico,
    cuius sit penitus nota fides animi,
meque esse inuenies illorum iure sacratum,
    Corneli, et factum me esse puta Harpocratem.

CIII

Avt sodes mihi redde decem sestertia, Silo,
    deinde esto quamuis saeuus et indomitus:
aut, si te numi delectant, desine quaeso
    leno esse atque idem saeuus et indomitus.

CIV

Credis me potuisse meae maledicere uitae,
    ambobus mihi quae carior est oculis?
non potui, nec, si possem, tam perdite amarem:
    sed tu cum Tappone omnia monstra facis.

CV

Mentvla conatur Pipleium scandere montem:
    Musae furcillis praecipitem eiciunt.

CVI

Cvm puero bello praeconem qui uidet isse,
    quid credat, nisi se uendere discupere?

CVII

Sı quoi quid cupido optantique optigit umquam
    insperanti, hoc est gratum animo proprie.
quare hoc est gratum †nobis quoque† carius auro
    quod te restituis, Lesbia, mi cupido.

restituis cupido atque insperanti, ipsa refers te
  nobis. o lucem candidiore nota!
quis me uno uiuit felicior, aut magis ab dis
  optandum in uita dicere quis poterit?

CVIII

Sɪ, Comini, arbitrio populi tua cana senectus
  spurcata impuris moribus intereat,
non equidem dubito quin primum inimica bonorum
  lingua excerpta auido sit data uulturio,
effossos oculos uoret atro gutture coruus,
  intestina canes, cetera membra lupi.

CIX

Ivcvɴᴅvм, mea uita, mihi proponis amorem
  hunc nostrum inter nos perpetuumque fore.
di magni, facite ut uere promittere possit,
  atque id sincere dicat et ex animo,
ut liceat nobis tota perducere uita
  aeternum hoc sanctae foedus amicitiae.

CX

Avꜰɪʟᴇɴᴀ, bonae semper laudantur amicae:
  accipiunt pretium, quae facere instituunt.
tu, quod promisti, mihi quod mentita inimica es,
  quod nec das nec fers, saepe facis facinus.
aut facere ingenuae est, aut non promisse pudicae,
  Aufilena, fuit: sed data corripere
fraudando effectis, plus quam meretricis auarae,
  quae sese toto corpore prostituit.

CXI

AVFILENA, uiro contentam uiuere solo,
nuptarum laus ex laudibus eximiis:
sed cuiuis quamuis potius succumbere par est,
quam matrem fratres ex patruo . . .

CXII

MVLTVS homo es, Naso, neque tecum multus homo qui
descendit: Naso, multus es et pathicus.

CXIII

CONSVLE Pompeio primum duo, Cinna, solebant
Maeciliam: facto consule nunc iterum
manserunt duo, sed creuerunt milia in unum
singula. fecundum semen adulterio.

CXIV

FIRMANVS saltu non falso Mentula diues
fertur, qui tot res in se habet egregias,
aucupium omne genus, piscis prata arua ferasque.
nequiquam: fructus sumptibus exsuperat.
quare concedo sit diues, dum omnia desint.
saltum laudemus, dum †modo† ipse egeat.

CXV

MENTVLA habet instar triginta iugera prati,
quadraginta arui: cetera sunt maria.
cur non diuitiis Croesum superare potis sit,
uno qui in saltu totmoda possideat,
prata arua ingentes siluas saltusque paludesque
usque ad Hyperboreos et mare ad Oceanum?
omnia magna haec sunt, tamen ipsest maximus ultro,
non homo, sed uero mentula magna minax.

CXVI

SAEPE tibi studioso animo uenante requirens
    carmina uti possem mittere Battiadae,
qui te lenirem nobis, neu conarere
    telis infestum mittere in usque caput,
hunc uideo mihi nunc frustra sumptum esse laborem,
    Gelli, nec nostras hic ualuisse preces.
contra nos tela ista tua euitamus amictei :
    at fixus nostris tu dabi supplicium.